DREAM JOURNEY

A SPIRITUAL GUIDE FOR PROFESSIONALIZING YOUR PASSION

RENEE DANIEL FLAGLER

Printed in the United States of America

First Edition October 2015

10 9 8 7 6 5 4 3 2 1

Library of Congress Control Number: 2020947532

❀ Created with Vellum

DEDICATION

I dedicate this book to the memory of Benny and Eva Daniel for allowing me to dream even when my dreams didn't make sense to them. Thank you for always having my back and being in my corner no matter what. Until we meet again…

CHAPTER 1

*I*t's not a destination. It's a journey.

I WALKED INTO THE SIZEABLE, non-descript building in the Mott Haven section of the Bronx, New York. Inside, I handed over my identification, emptied my pockets, and stuffed my belongings into a small locker. With the officer's approval behind the thick bulletproof partition, I was allowed entry through a set of massive steel doors that shut with a frightening sense of finality. I knew I'd only be here for an hour, but still, I cringed every single time I heard the sound of those enormous steel doors closing behind me, locking me in. On the other side, I waited for another officer to escort me through the stark, sterile corridors to the open area where I met with a dozen young incarcerated youth every week.

I facilitated writing workshops at a juvenile detention center and several other facilities housing youth in unfortunate situations. Depending on the day of the week, I worked with young men and women in group homes, alternative schools, jails, and even drug treatment centers. After several weeks, I'd grown particularly fond of one group of young men. They embraced what I was eager to teach. We explored, dissected, and discussed poetry in every possible form, starting with rap lyrics using artists like Tupac, Common, and Arrested Development. Later, I presented them with more renowned classics like Langston Hughes, Nikki Giovani, Lucile Clifton, and more. We talked about metaphors, similes, personification, and other types of figurative language. We examined themes, voice, and the poet's intent. There I was, locked down inside a prison with stuffy cells along the perimeter of the space we occupied, escaping into worlds created by masterful writers. These young men and I tried to emulate the masters with our own experiences.

Several of these boys were genuinely gifted. They exhibited extreme poetic talent and had written some of the most profound poems and lyrics I'd ever experienced. They had seen and been through so much in their young lives and had so much to say.

During one particular session my goal was to explore the idea of pursuing dreams. I started the lesson by playing the song *If I Ruled the World* by Nas to open their minds about what could be possible in life. Once again, the goal was to lift them out of the confines of their surroundings and expand their vision. I dared them to dream. I asked them to visualize a moment in the future that would define the fact that they had 'made it.' One young man who I will call Terrance excitedly described his moment of playing basketball and shooting a winning three-point shot.

He painted a compelling picture: The score is tied. There are seconds left in the game. The clock is quickly counting down. The crowd is on their feet. Terrance dribbles, takes the ball in his hands and zeroes in on the hoop. Sweat trickles down his forehead. His heart beat violently against his chest. He knows how important this shot is. He bends his knee. The tension in the arena thickens. He takes several breaths and steadies his hands. With the most precision he could manage, he tosses the ball. There is a collective gasp. The room plummets into a deafening silence and everyone holds their breath. All eyes are on the ball as it soars through the air. It's like it's moving in slow motion. It takes forever. Finally, it sinks right into the basket. All net! The crowd erupts, applauding, and cheering. His teammates lift him into the air above their heads and chant in victory.

Terrance was starry-eyed as he told his story. He seemed to be transported inside his dream. He was there in that arena, hearing the crowd, feeling the victory, celebrating his big win. It seemed real. He smiled—a fresh, authentic, freeing smile. I'd never seen him so happy.

Several other young men had similar experiences that day. It was exhilarating. While we embraced the excitement that visualizing dreams brought, I moved the lesson to talk about how dreams were more than individual pivotal moments or experiences. We talked about how dreams were journeys filled with moments just like the one Terrance described, and with ebbs and flows, wins, and failures. We talked about how vital the losses were because they taught us the most. The defining moment in that session was when I told them that the moment they decide to embark on the pursuit of their dream, is when their dream journey begins.

Terrance's brows furrowed. A pensive look covered his face. After a while, he asked, "Even here?" And that's when I believe he truly got it. I told him yes, even here in this place, a juvenile detention center, even in jail. I explained that this was only a stopover and that he would learn so much in this season of life that would help him in the next. I told him if he developed a plan that would get him to that pivotal moment, and so many others, all he needed to do was take one step at a time, and he could get there.

"Terrance, the moment you take that first step, you've started your journey. With focus, the possibilities are endless."

The idea that the mistakes he'd made to land him in a juvenile detention center didn't have to determine the outcome of his entire life freed Terrance's mind that day. By the time we completed our weekly sessions, Terrance had figured out a few things that he could do while he was still in the detention center, and after his release, that would help him achieve his dreams. That lesson permitted him to dream again. And because he could begin taking simple steps immediately, like planning and visualizing, the dream didn't seem so far away and unattainable. The dream felt closer to him. It felt possible. This kid finally dared to dream.

Not every kid in the program dared to dream in the way that Terrance did. Terrance represents the person that this book was written for. He was an example of those who dared to dream and something about the dream caught hold of them and wouldn't let go. Terrance represents the unique swath of the people who feel like something is missing in their lives, but perhaps they can' t put their finger on exactly what it is. They want to explore it. They desire to finally move into a state of knowing, and understanding that would make a difference in how the rest of their lives plays out.

We are the folks with a dream that's been so tightly woven into our DNA that it separates us from feeling comfortable simply settling into the day-to-day stuff of the world....and we don't know what to do with that, or about that, but we're willing to take our chances and take action. It's at this point that we experience a yearning to explore the possibilities and delve into unchartered territory.

What is a Dream Journey Anyway?

I define it as a life that is inspired by the pursuit of one's passion. It's a life journey fueled by one's dreams. It's a journey that ebbs and flows with successes and failures, wins and losses that all add up to a fantastic odyssey. It requires that you recognize your wins, both big and small, and pause long enough to take notice of how far you've come, and then celebrate. It requires that you learn from your pitfalls instead of wallowing in them. These lessons help you change the necessary behaviors and ideas to help you do better and be better. Collectively, all of this together makes you better. It's being around people who encourage and support your goals. It's using your time and resources to get you closer to your goals and those monumental moments. The journey is filled with pivotal moments. These moments link together to create the arc, and the story of your journey. Ultimately, a dream journey becomes your lifestyle.

Most people don't think of pursuing their dream as a lifestyle. Nor do they usually consider that the steps they need to take to realize their dreams are a lifestyle change when, in fact, it is just that. Merriam-Webster defines lifestyle as the typical way of life of an individual, group, or culture. Though there may not be anything ordinary about pursuing one's dream, a life inspired by a particular pursuit is *a way of life.* Take spirituality, for example. People who consider themselves spiritual operate within a culture of spirituality. Their experiences include actions, activities, and routines that are aligned with what they believe. Some pray daily, whether it's once or several times a day. Sabbath observances include attending their designated houses of worship, participating in various worship experiences, and engaging with people that do the same things. Often, their family and closest friends participate in similar spiritual practices. Their spirituality is a critical thread that weaves different parts of their lives together. It prominently influences their decisions, the people they keep around them, the money they spend, and how they use their time and other resources.

Many factors influence one's lifestyle. Despite what those

factors are, it's easy to identify someone's way of life by how they spend their time and resources and respond to the things in life that are most important to them. If sports are essential to an individual, they likely spend time watching sports on television, attending sports events, purchasing sports paraphernalia, and keeping up with what's happening in and around the world of sports. Often, their family members and closest friends share their love of sports and spend the same amount of time and resources engaged in that world.

I could exchange categories like spirituality and sports for almost any area of interest, such as fitness, art, travel, and yes, even dreams. The critical thing to know is that our 'way of life' is always inspired by our values. What we value determines our choices. And our choices influence how we interact with the world. As another example, fitness buffs spend lots of time getting fit, they purchase more workout gear than the average person, consistently learn about new fitness options, and gravitate to people who look, think, spend, act and live as they do.

People who actively live in the pursuit of their dreams are the same way. We put time and money into what we're pursuing. These are the things that interest us the most. We gravitate to like-minded people who are also inspired to live by the pursuit of their dreams. There are things we will do and won't do solely based on what we desire. We make sacrifices for our goals. We value our dreams. Our dreams influence us. We are inspired by our dreams and make choices based on our plans. We find comfort in the community of other dreamers. These actions, this way of living, dictates a lifestyle. An artist may love shoes, but because they are so inspired by their artsy lifestyle, they are more likely to use their financial resources to purchase art supplies than another pair of shoes. Their lifestyle influences their purchasing decisions.

Lifestyle choices set us apart from other people in the same way that our dreams set us apart. The dream is where it all starts. Somewhere inside us there's a nudge in our gut that grows if we pay enough attention to ourselves to recognize it. The first indication is often a feeling. It's abstract and not always easy to identify. Therefore, people don't know what to do about them. The nudges and desires come and go based on external forces that stimulate them. That is why dreams are usually ignored. Sometimes they're downright scary to some people and written off as silly ideas or impossible notions. Dreams can't manifest under those terms. Too often, people won't allow themselves to indulge in the folly of imagining. But imagination is often the fertile ground through which dreams manifest. Dreams nudge us, hoping we will give them the consideration they need to begin to develop. When we pay attention to our desires and allow them to come forth in some manner, we realize that dreams are the seeds of our passions. Our passions compel and drive us. Our passions are much more forceful than our dreams, and always leave more concrete clues.

Yes, Passion Leaves Clues

I gathered a forum of eleven women for research in the development of this book. Each of these women are living their Dream Journey—lives inspired by the pursuit of their passions. As most like-minded groups of people living similar lifestyles, these women had so many shared experiences, even though every one of them had a different career path. One of the first commonalities we were able to identify is that they all had a dream connected with their passion.

Initially, none of them realized this connection. Yet, every woman reached a point where they could no longer ignore or deny the profound desire to give in to their passions. They were able to look back and realize those dreams and passions had always been with them, leaving clues across the span of their lives.

Dr. Michele Reed is one of the eleven women that I interviewed. She's a physician that runs a family practice with two locations. Her earliest memory of her desire to be in the field of medicine dated back to when she was four years old. Dr. Reed was intrigued by doctors from their white coats to their stethoscopes. She dreamed of becoming a doctor when she grew up. Over time, Dr. Reed realized that she had a passion for medicine and a natural propensity towards the field and a certain proficiency level.

Allowing your passion to blossom, manifest into your dream and influence your life is what living your dream is all about. However, this book takes things a step further. Not only do I want you to dream, realize your dream, indulge your passion and live out your life's purpose, I also want to help you begin living a life inspired by your dreams. I want you to immerse yourself in your passion and fully walk in your purpose. I want you to eat, breathe, love, laugh, play, and work wrapped in your love. And I want you to get paid while doing it.

CHAPTER 2

Your Journey Starts Here

DON'T you just love it when you're looking for directions, and you come across a kiosk and see the words, "You Are Here?" There are times when I've said aloud, "Where is here?" Even with that bit of direction, starting a new journey or hitting a crossroads along the way can leave you wondering where to start or where to go next. Getting your bearings can be frustrating or exciting, frightening, or thrilling, confusing, or enlightening. Regardless of what feelings emerge, take comfort in knowing that your journey has begun, and give yourself credit for getting further than where you were when you started.

Whether you purchased this book yourself or someone bought it for you, you're here for a reason. You believe there's more to life. Perhaps you feel like something is missing. You want to live more meaningfully. You possess a passion for something. You have a dream. Maybe you know your passion or want to take your passion and run your life with it. Regardless of what brought you to the pages of this book, you are ready for more. You want to go to the next step. Some people go through life pushing their passions aside. Others simply can't. These people are a unique swath of the population whose passion is just too strong to be ignored. It's like a fire burning in your gut that refuses to be doused, leaving you no choice but to give it your undivided attention.

You've already determined there's something different about you. There's something you're seeking. You're ready for a change. A transformation is in store. You can feel it bubbling in your spirit. You can't put your finger on it. It's intangible, yet it lives and breathes, inspires, and moves inside of you. You've always been different.

Growing up, you played with friends just like most kids. As an adult, you interacted with many groups of people, but for some reason, you never quite felt like you truly fit in with any of them. Many times it bothered you—You believed it was your fault. You assessed yourself and wondered why. In a room full of people you sometimes still felt alone. At times you cared. Other times you didn't. Hopefully, one day it started not to matter so much. You did well being alone because you found comfort in your own space.

Yes! You are different. That's why fitting in can feel so uncomfortable. It's great to find common ground with the people in your life. Having things in common helps us relate to others, but that doesn't change the fact that you're supposed to stand out. That burning desire to veer off the path of what you see as common is what leads you toward the life that brings you fulfillment.

You are wired and equipped to carry out your dreams, meaning you already have the natural gifts, talents, and abilities that you would need to live out your dreams. For example, artists are equipped with an innate ability to create art. What often follows is a desire to create art. When artists indulge their desire to create, they experience a sense of fulfillment. They will become driven by that sense of fulfillment to create and seek out opportunities to engage in this passion that they've developed more often. Visual artists like painters don't go to school to learn how to paint. They go to develop their skills, fine-tune and hone their craft and or gain credentials. I'm far from being a painter, and no matter how many classes I take, I will never be better. My DNA wasn't equipped with the painter's strand.

Some of our gifts are easier to recognize, and some are not so easy. Gifts may be hidden behind things that bring us joy. For example, musical talents are easy to identify, but someone's innate ability to make a person feel better about themselves may not be as evident. An individual may be able to lift someone's spirits in a way that others can't and they will obtain immense joy from helping people. Despite what one's gift or talent may be or how evident it is, joy rises in us when we're operating in our gift or talent. When nurtured, that joy manifests as passion. Passions shed light on our innate gifts and talents and serve as the catalyst that compels us into action. They are also the vehicles that fuel our dreams and drive us toward our purpose.

It's the natural gift that first gives light to our dreams. As with most people, my Dream Journey started well before I realized it. I was a terrific shock—the unexpected last kid of six children with a five-year gap between my brother and me. My parents assumed they were done having kids, but I had other plans. There was even a joke by one of my mother's family members to name me Quits, insinuating that after my birth, my parents should consider quitting the baby-making game. My older siblings were in elementary, middle, and high school when I came along—the oldest two were just about ready to graduate.

As a young person, I never felt like I fit in. Not even at home.

I was the youngest of six children, and my desires were always completely different from anything my parents and siblings ever thought about. I'd tell my mother about things I wanted to do, the places I wanted to go, and the life I wanted to live, and she'd just say, 'Okay, baby.' She never discouraged me. But she didn't encourage me either. I don't know if she believed that I even knew what I was talking about. Neither did she question me—at first. I assume she chucked it all up to an active imagination. My sisters and brother were different. They'd scrunch their noses, gape at me with wide eyes, and say things like, "Why do you want to do that? No one in our family has ever done that." That fact that I was grazing toward unchartered territory enticed me even more.

I wanted—no, I needed to see the world before I had any idea what the world consisted of. My favorite way to explore this unknown world was through books. I developed a relationship with words. When I think back, my earliest and clearest memory of falling in love with words was when I memorized an entire book in the second grade. I recited it during an assembly in a storytelling contest in front of the whole second grade. I won the competition and went on to represent my school at the district level. I didn't win there, but I realized that more remarkable things were possible. Memorizing that book and winning that contest was one of the first encounters I had with my passion. The memory stays with me to this day. Now I realize that my victory in that storytelling competition was a clue left by my passion to help me find the way to my dream.

I also discovered that I was good at communications, reading, writing, and talking. I talked a lot and moved even more. It was almost impossible for me to stand still. Energy coursed through me all the time. I couldn't recount the many times my mother stopped what she was doing, looked at me and said, "Stop all that jumping." Until she said that, I hadn't even realized I was jumping around.

As a child, I stood in front of the mirror giving speeches, entertaining imaginary audiences, and then made noises with my mouth to resemble their adoring cheers. Reading and writing incredibly imaginative stories was another favorite pastime. Later, I became enamored with people who authored books. Authors have always been my celebrities. Judy Blume is still one of my favorites. I didn't know then that I was exercising my gifts for use much later in life. When I look back, I realize that these were clues that my passion left behind—a trail leading from the very first time I indulged my passion to the day I realized it. These were also the things that isolated me from my siblings and friends and united me with others who shared the same interests. My siblings didn't share the same love for talking, reading, and writing that I did. Arguably, my imagination was a bit wilder than theirs. I looked at life through the lens of possibilities. Reality did not excite me.

It wasn't until I was much older that I became less bothered that those around me didn't share my desires. My siblings, other family members, teachers, and my friends' mothers told me I was different. Even the Bible speaks to the fact that we are all uniquely crafted. Ephesians 3:10 says, *"For we are God's workmanship, created in Jesus Christ for good works, which God prepared beforehand that we should walk in them." NKJV.* I was designed for what I was to do. However, in my teens and throughout my twenties, I learned to keep my 'differences' under wrap and try my best to fit in, but it never truly worked. Eventually, I grew comfortable with who I was and owned that identity.

The funny thing about who you are is that the real you never goes away. No matter how hard I tried to blend in, my differences still stood out. Some folks saw it clearly, and made comments. Others didn't seem to notice. I didn't appreciate what made me distinct until it started to benefit me. Somehow, I became the person everyone came to when they wanted to write something compelling, whether it was a note, cover letter for a job, resume, or a letter about lousy customer service. I helped pen many of those. I once wrote a four-page letter to a bank expressing my dissatisfaction with their customer service. I was a struggling young adult who hadn't developed good financial management skills yet. The financial institution confirmed receipt of my letter with a letter of their own, apologizing for my 'stress and inconvenience.' That letter made an impact. I swear they must have tagged my account somehow, because after that, I received better customer service than I ever had in my life.

By my thirties, I'd written almost everything there was to write; screenplays, books, songs, marketing, advertising materials, website content, magazine and newsletter articles, and even obituaries for people I'd never met. Everyone else seemed to know that I wrote well. I didn't think much of it. I was simply doing something that came easy to me. And yes, I enjoyed doing it.

I wrote all the time. When I graduated from film school but decided I didn't want to go into that industry, I turned screenplays into books. I wasn't writing for publication at the time. I wrote because I enjoyed writing. It was therapeutic for me. If I had a bad day, bad things happened to my characters. If I had a good day, great things happened in my stories. I created opportunities to write at work. One time I suggested we start a newsletter and who ended up writing all of the articles? Me.

I was a marketing manager. People at work came to me so I could help them wordsmith letters and emails. I became the go-to person for all things written with the people in my life, both personally and professionally. I didn't know that my passion for writing was making its way to the surface. Eventually, that passion outright inspired many of the decisions in my life.

I had an appreciation for all kinds of writing, and journalism intrigued me. I'd taken some classes in college and held a strong affinity for magazines. I had monthly subscriptions for ten to fifteen different magazines and believed I could do what the writers of those articles were doing. In 2000 I reached out to several of my favorite publications to inquire about writing for them. By the next month, I received my first writing assignment as a freelance journalist and wrote for them and other notable publications for more than fifteen years. I even won an *Excellence in Journalism* award from the New York Chapter of the National Association of Black Journalists.

Of all of these types of writing, creative writing remained my favorite. I devoured books and soon believed I could do what those authors were doing, create stories that pulled people right into the pages and made them feel like they were there with the characters experiencing the story as it played out. I decided to try it for myself.

Initially, I came up with several stories. As soon as an idea popped into my head I'd start laying out a new storyline. After a while, I had several unfinished manuscripts. I didn't have any plans beyond developing the stories. I wasn't concerned about getting published or becoming an author. I was simply doing something I enjoyed. Again, it was therapeutic. For many years, I wrote for the pure joy of it.

Meanwhile, as a budding manager, I was well into my career as a rising marketing professional with my eyes on the C-suite. One day I would bear the title of Chief Marketing Officer. I was sure of it. Although my core focus was marketing, I consistently incorporated writing into the jobs I held. I wrote website content, newsletters, articles, sales kits, emails, conference registration forms, sponsorship materials, ads, brochures, etc. You name it. I wrote it. While still writing freelance for several publications, I created fictional stories in my spare time until something devastating happened.

For the first time in my life, I got laid off. It happened a month after the horrific events of 9/11. Many of our vendors and customers were directly impacted by the terrorist attacks.

Complete companies were wiped out. Some simply never recovered from their immeasurable losses. No less than thirty days later, our company slashed the workforce in half, eliminating positions from administrative assistants to vice presidents. Our competitors met similar fates. The industry dubbed the massive job slashings a 'blood bath.' At that point, all I had left was writing, but it wasn't enough to pay any bills.

With no job to report to each morning, I filled my days by engaging in an intense search for my next opportunity. In the meantime, I continued writing and began taking on more freelance assignments. I freelanced for a year until I was able to secure another marketing job. I quickly learned, on a very personal level, how hard the attacks of 9/11 impacted our economy. Marketing and advertising were the first two budgets to get cut when companies had to reduce expenses. Finding and sustaining a career in this arena became too challenging.

Finally, I secured another position as a marketing manager. I assumed that if I continued to work hard, I could secure my job by becoming indispensable. I consistently went above and beyond my duties. I often spoke and or emceed at our events, gaining the attention of top clients. I built great relationships with vendors and wore various hats. Yet, less than six months later, I found myself unemployed again.

This time, the blow to my professional ego landed even harder. At a time when I should have been climbing the corporate ladder and gaining the contacts and credentials I needed to make it to that C-suite, I just couldn't seem to keep a job. I came equipped with a bachelor's and master's degree, was a team-player, and a hard worker who was willing to take the initiative, roll up my sleeves, and do what was necessary to get the job done. Where had I gone wrong?

I questioned everything I'd learned about what it took to pave a professional path for success. I questioned myself. Was I good enough? Were there skills I lacked without realizing it?

Did I need to go back to school—again? Suddenly, I was no longer confident in my background and abilities. This layoff lasted longer than the previous one. Weekdays, from 9 am to 5 pm, I was glued to my computer, searching job boards to find a job. For months, my search yielded no results. I had a few interviews, but no job offers. To fill the pending gap building in my resume, I took low-paying consulting gigs helping entrepreneurs develop marketing plans while taking on more freelance assignments. The only time I felt valuable was when I spent time with my family, or when I was writing.

I was proud of my education, but questioned if going 'all the way' to acquire that master's degree had made any difference. I was over-qualified for the available positions. Potential employers stated that 'despite my impressive qualifications, unfortunately, I had not been chosen for the position.' My collection of rejection letters grew. With each failed attempt at securing employment, my confidence crumbled just a little bit more. Eventually, I questioned if I'd made the right decision in choosing a career in marketing altogether. I enjoyed the work because it allowed me to be creative, and the ability to express my creativity is what I wanted most.

After feeling particularly broken, I prayed and asked God what I was 'supposed' to do. There were so many things I liked. And because I loved learning, I found opportunities to gain more and more knowledge every time I discovered an exciting new interest. Besides my degrees, I'd taken certificate courses in various programs and took classes to learn all kinds of things. I'd replaced my time being unemployed with just being busy. Essentially, I was all over the place. I had to do something— anything. It pained me to see my husband work so hard to single-handedly try to make ends meet on one salary after we'd built a lifestyle that was solidly dependent on two incomes.

Daily, I prayed for inspiration and guidance. It was the most I could do. I needed God to help me focus. I had to know where to direct my time and energy because it was evident that what I had been doing so far wasn't working. Before this, I had never considered turning to Him regarding my career. Before this, I had reserved God for Sundays.

During this time I continued reading. I continued writing. I continued looking for a new job, but I was also searching for my place in life. I was at that place in front of the kiosk that said, "You Are Here," but I had no idea where "Here" was.

I was in my thirties. I had expected to reach several professional milestones by then. I thought I would be in an executive position. Instead, I felt like I had taken several steps backwards. Despite all my efforts, I still had no job and no prospects. I wasn't earning enough money with my side efforts to make any real impact at home with the bills. I was overworked, spinning my wheels, tired and frustrated. When I looked around, it didn't appear that any other family members or friends were dealing with any of the issues I was dealing with. I was the one that was supposed to 'make it', to be successful, to reach levels and heights never seen before amongst my family. I had gone the farthest in school even though I was the youngest child in my family.

Slowly, my interest in all the things I was doing to earn money started to dissipate. I focused on finding a job. Outside of that, I wrote. Writing was the only interest that remained.

I spent the next several years getting new jobs and getting laid off shortly after. I finally landed another opportunity at a large company that published magazines and journals and produced significant conferences and events. I had attended some of those conferences while employed in my previous positions. Being fully qualified, I applied for the position and was called in for an interview. The job seemed simple enough, but several things about it made me feel like this wasn't the right opportunity. Desperate to collect a check and be able to once again contribute to my household financially, I took the position when it was offered.

Once I started, there was never any real clarity around my title or job responsibilities. I never felt like my skills were being fully utilized. I had so much that I wanted to contribute, but many of my ideas were blatantly pushed aside. One month later, my boss, who had been hired with me, called in and quit. Her abrupt departure made me wonder if I should consider leaving too. With just a month in, if I left, I wouldn't have had to put that job on my resume. However, I needed the money. After my boss's resignation I reported directly to the Chief Marketing Officer, which was initially exciting. That was the title I had my eye on. I was prepared to learn as much from her as possible. However, she hardly spoke to me. I was left floundering, trying to figure out a way to make a meaningful contribution to the team, my department, and the company as a whole. I needed to make my position relevant because, at that point, I felt dispensable. I was dispensable, and knew that sooner or later, everyone would realize it.

Several months into the position, nothing had changed. I'd built some relationships, but none of them were within my department. I felt like my days were numbered. Once again, I was potentially facing the possibility of being unemployed, and my husband and I had yet to climb out of the financial hardship created by my first two layoffs. Despite the uncertainly, I reported to work every single day. As I hit the elevator call button, I'd say, "I'm getting a check." That was my primary—actually, my only, reason for getting on that elevator. I'd ascend to my floor, make my way through the day, and try to feel valuable. I needed a job. I had one, regardless of how unfulfilling it was. I tried my best to feel grateful.

By 2004 my job searches continued to yield minimal results. My goal was to find something gratifying. Something that made me look forward to getting up and going to work every day at a place where I could make a valuable contribution. I needed something that felt like an extension of who I was. This next job couldn't just be any kind of job. It had to be *the* job. I decided to stay in my position until that ideal opportunity came along, hoping it would happen before another possible lay off.

In the meantime, I made the best of my situation. Before the summer ended, I attended a company picnic and met a woman named Susan Herriot. Following an afternoon of team building, food, and activities, we found that we had a lot in common. Susan and I became fast friends after finding out that we were both avid readers who happened to be fond of some of the same authors. Both of us had roots in Queens, New York.

Susan worked within the department that published journals on a different floor. After the picnic, we'd often get together for lunch. Books were always part of our conversations. During one of these lunch outings, I'd expressed to Susan that I had an interest in writing and had begun working on several stories. Susan asked if she could read some of my work. Excited to share with a fellow reader and experienced editor, I brought in several chapters of one of the books I was working on. The story I chose to share with Susan was one I had started many years before. It was now my primary therapeutic escape during the recent periods of unemployment even though I still wasn't giving much thought to getting anything published.

A week later, Susan and I met for lunch. She raved about what she'd read and insisted that I had a 'marketable page-turner' on my hands. Susan encouraged me to try to get the book published once it was finished. That was the first time I seriously considered being an author. Susan shared any information she could find about the process of getting published. This reinvigorated my desire to write. I began doing research and reached out to publishing houses, authors, bookstores, libraries, and continuing education programs for insight, and I started my search for a literary agent.

I shared my research with my brother, Rodney, who also had an interest in writing. Rodney encouraged me to look into self-publishing as an option. That sent me down a new path of research. I found information on both independent and traditional publishing, compared the two, and decided to try my hand at publishing the book on my own.

The uncertainty of my job no longer seemed as daunting. I went to work every day looking forward to getting together with Susan to talk about what I'd found out about getting published, or to share the new chapters I'd written. Despite not feeling valued at work, this new endeavor was fulfilling. Writing gave me immense joy. Engaging in this new world around writing was energizing in a way that I'd never experienced before. After spending time with my husband and young son, I'd stay up well into the night writing or researching publishing. During that time I realized writing was more than just something I liked to do in my spare time. I was passionate about writing and everything that had anything to do with it. And then it happened—again.

Late one morning I received a call at my desk asking that I meet the Chief Marketing Office in the conference room. I'd been there before and knew what was about to happen. I didn't feel the same sense of dread or disappointment I had on the two previous occasions. I stood confidently, held my head high, my chest out, and stepped into that conference room ready to be released into the next phase of my life.

My boss, the chief marketing officer, sat beside a sad-faced woman from the human resources department. I walked in slowly and sat opposite the two of them, separated by a bulky, dominating conference table. My boss sat stoically and began delivering her spiel about the department's reorganization, having to make cuts, and a small severance that I'd be entitled to receive. I wasn't upset, and surprisingly, I didn't feel betrayed as I had during my last layoff. Instead, I sat half-smiling. The HR executive seemed more upset about what was happening than I was.

At this point, I was practically a pro at being laid off. My boss apologized and insisted that this decision wasn't personal, but it was— "I jumped in to finish her sentence with, "as per the needs of the business." She nodded. Then she said, "Please know that you can always—" Again, I interrupted and finished her sentence with, "I know, use you as a reference." After a few more of these, I told them I understood, giving them more comfort than they tried to give me. I practically laid myself off for them. When it was all over, I thanked them for offering me the opportunity to use them as references for my next position. I left, leaving them both looking a bit puzzled. By the time I made it back to my office, I felt free.

I said goodbye to a few people I'd grown fond of, grabbed my belongings, and headed home. I may have even skipped on my way out. I called my husband and before he could say hello I yelled, "Guess what? I got laid off!" My poor husband couldn't speak. His only response was a deafening silence.

Meanwhile, excitement bubbled in my chest. "And…that's a good thing?" he finally asked when he found his voice. After all we'd been through, after so much struggling, he couldn't understand how I could deliver that news with so much enthusiasm. We still hadn't climbed out of our financial hole. At home lay stacks of bills, and our credit score was free-falling due to our inability to make ends meet. My poor husband thought I had lost my mind. Fortunately, he knew the dreamer he had married, and assumed I had a plan.

I knew exactly how I would spend the days following my layoff. Tears and job boards weren't part of the plan this time. That night, I shared my desires with my husband. I couldn't contain my exhilaration. I finally realized that I didn't write because I liked it. It was my passion. I was sure about that now. This was something I had to do, or else I'd spend a lifetime in regret. Something powerful propelled me forward, confirmed that this was the appropriate next step. It scared and excited me. Instead of succumbing to fear, I let that energy fuel my motivation and dreamed about the possibilities.

My two previous layoffs taught me that I could survive on a lower household income. We already knew how to hunker down and live on a budget. I didn't have to just depend on collecting a check and living unfulfilled. A sacrifice was required. Austerity would become a way of life. Something deep inside confirmed for me that I was making the right move. This was my chance. This was my time. My husband supported me and offered to do whatever was needed to help me pursue this dream.

I woke the next morning ready to get started. That day and the next thirty days after that I got up every weekday morning, took my son to school, went back home, and wrote until it was time to pick him up at the end of his day. Within the month, I'd finished my first novel and started the journey to self-publish my first book. Susan Herriot was my first editor.

To sum this up, I had a gift, which was writing. I experienced joy whenever I wrote. The joy made me want to write as often as I could. I accepted the fact that this was a passion. Being passionate about writing led to exploring ways that I do it more often. I dreamed about becoming a professional writer. It took years for me to get from having a gift, and recognizing that gift, to dreaming about the possibilities and actually operating in that dream. However, once I began to dream, my desire to fulfill that dream was the catalyst that changed the course of my life.

HERE

During this process, I discovered something valuable. I was equipped for my journey. I finally knew where I was. When the layoff happened, I'd reached a crossroad. I could head home and search for another unfulfilling job, or I could pursue this passion of mine and see where it could take me. The whole idea of forging forward into uncharted territory both frightened and thrilled me. Despite the fear, I couldn't turn back. I had to take this chance. The desire to push forward had settled deep in my bones. It was risky. It was different. There was so much to be concerned about, but I had to do it. If it didn't work out, I could always go back to working in marketing. But I didn't want that.

I decided that I'd rather fail trying than to not try at all. So with little money, my husband by my side, and loads of imaginative hope, I gathered my talents and abilities and headed towards the unknown.

This was my leap of faith. I'd jumped off that proverbial cliff and waited for God to catch me and carry me toward success. And what was success? At that point I didn't know, but I was looking forward to navigating my way toward finding out.

Prior to this pivotal experience, I had grown bitter with corporate America. I had even been a little angry with the world for leading me to believe that a good education, a few degrees, and lots of hard work would guarantee me a certain sense of security. Like I said, there I was with two degrees and couldn't seem to keep a job. I was in unemployment lines right alongside people who had no high school diplomas. I was struggling to make ends meet just like any other person trying to maintain a hold on the elusive American Dream. What a humbling experience.

My inability to help make ends meet at times caused me to experience deep shame. The fact that I wasn't able to live up to the success people had grown to expect from me was embarrassing. I fought depression. I felt guilty that my inability to remain gainfully employed caused such a burden for my household. I kept a smile on my face despite what I was going through until I realized the value of all that I had endured.

I realized that every trial I had endured up to this point,

including the layoff, was a set up that proved to me I could make it. This experience put things into perspective. We struggled financially, but still managed to keep our home and put food on the table. We weren't able to join our friends on vacations, but we found less expensive ways to engage in family fun. We ate out less and lived on austerity. I found out what it was like to creatively make things work with less income. I became extremely resourceful and was eventually able to fill in some financial gaps.

Most importantly, I realized that by cutting back and being smart and efficient, our household could make it without me receiving a steady check. At that point, we'd survived a few years. So I stopped whining and starting paying more attention to what I needed to learn about my experiences.

I learned what was important. I learned how to sacrifice. I learned how to work with what I had. I learned efficiency. I learned how to be innovative. I learned that I didn't want to just have a job. I wanted to live out my passion. I wanted to find a way to make my passion work for me. I wanted to get paid doing what I loved. I'd heard those ideas before, "Do what you love, and you'll never work a day in your life." For the first time, this made complete sense to me. I liked marketing. I didn't love it. I loved writing and everything associated with it. I decided I was going to do what I loved, and I was going to find a way to get paid for it. I knew that this was going to be an adventure, and I couldn't wait to take my next step.

I stepped into my dream fully. I made the intentional and informed decision to pursue it. I made the necessary changes to my life in order to make it possible. I embraced the gifts I had to make my new life possible. The hold that my dream had on me wouldn't allow me to go back to living the way I used to despite the sacrifices I had to make. The realization of my dreams finally seemed tangible and I wanted the life that I'd imagined pursuing my dreams would provide for me. It wasn't about money. It was about fulfillment and passion. I also knew that I could fail, but I knew the experience would be worth the risk.

You are here! You're reading this book. You're in position. You can start from right where you are with what you already have. It's your time. Take what you've got in your hand and take that next step.

CHAPTER 3

It's Not All About You

I DID IT. I jumped off the cliff. Instead of running back to the alleged security of another job, I made the commitment to give my passion a chance. My publishing career started with pure enthusiasm and theory. I quickly learned how hard it really was to become a published author—specifically a self-published author. Every myth I'd ever put stock into was busted within the first six months. This thing required lots of hard work, thick skin, and numerous nights of getting little sleep. The initial payback was fatigue coupled with hardly any money. I also knew that I was not supposed to give up.

There was no magical formula, and I was okay with that. I'd worked hard for many companies—getting up early, working long grueling days, and sometimes getting paid very little in return. These companies didn't have a problem separating with me after giving them my all. So, if I could work hard for them, I could certainly work hard for myself. I wasn't disillusioned after those first six months. I understood this would be a huge learning experience. I knew it would take time. I also realized that people didn't write books and become rich and famous Over night.There was no such thing as an overnight success.

I threw myself completely into my new world, learning to understand the business, getting in front of readers and eventually finding my tribe. I made mistakes—huge ones. What I found most interesting is that every single experience up to that point, including the skills I developed in corporate positions and during my times of unemployment, became glaringly relevant. Not only did I use the talents and gifts that were in my DNA, but everything I learned in college and during my career in marketing became useful. All the ups and downs I'd experienced to this point prepared me for what I was doing. Working jobs in the past that I didn't enjoy helped me appreciate being able to get up each day and do something that brought me pure joy. Living without a steady paycheck showed me that there was more to life than just getting a check.

I knew I had to do this for me, and also realized I had to do this for other people around me as well. When I first told my mother about my desire to become a writer instead of going back to work, she thought I had lost my mind. She couldn't understand why I had made such a frivolous decision. It seemed like too much to accomplish. She'd never personally met a successful writer. In fact, no one in my entire family had, and they were all nervous for me. Some applauded my bravery while others warned me against it. Some talked behind my back about how I was unfair to my husband for subjecting him to becoming the single breadwinner in the house. I was ridiculed for what 'they' called putting my husband in a position to have to care for all of our financial needs on his own. Others wondered, 'Who did I think I was to believe this was something I could achieve?' I tuned out all of the negative talk and allowed the positive reinforcement to fuel my persistence. I was going to do this or fail trying.

Fortunately for me, my husband was my biggest cheerleader. Next to my mother, he was my most staunch supporter. When I shared my dream with him, he all but insisted I give it a try. We buckled down on our household expenses to make things work. We skipped outings, events, and trips to avoid spending money. Household expenses were scaled down to the bare minimum. My husband and I lived in austerity. Some months the ends didn't quite meet, and some months they did. There were times when my immediate family members helped us get along. They believed the sacrifices were worth it. It was no-frills living. Despite our scarce existence, we were arguably the happiest we'd ever been.

I was excited about my work every single day. Together, my husband and I celebrated the small accomplishments and the huge, memorable accomplishments. This part of the journey was filled with so much discovery. I learned about the industry, people, writing, and myself. I even created a conference for other self-published authors where key industry professionals from all sides of the publishing business came together to teach our audience about best practices. This helped me to not only learn more about the business I was in, but it also helped me establish amazing relationships with fellow authors, publishers, agents, and media professionals—many of whom I'm still very close with to this day.

A year later, I was still excited about my life. It was worth missing trips and living scarcely. The benefits couldn't be measured by dollar signs. Some people around us still wondered if all the sacrifices we were making made sense. Some applauded my resolve and willingness to stick it out. Personally, despite the amount of money I used to make in my corporate jobs, I couldn't see myself going back.

My mother, Eva Daniel, was a practical woman who lived

for her children. She made practical decisions with nearly guaranteed outcomes—decisions that were safe and certain for the security of her six kids. My father, Benny Daniel, encouraged us a bit more to chart new territories but was still a very practical man that taught his children that familiar adage, "Find yourself a good job and work hard." He'd often tell us, "I don't care if you're a street sweeper, be the best damn street sweeper there is. If you can't be *the* best, then be *one of the* best." My parents, like many of their generation, wanted us to put stock into 'good jobs,' and for some reason, I wasn't willing to invest in that idea. I wanted something different. There was more in me—more for me to do. I knew this, but wasn't sure how to get more out of me. I didn't mind being the first in my family to see what life could be like outside the box of working a 'good job' until I retired. That wasn't going to cut it for me. It left way too many unexplored opportunities off the table.

My parents were practical, but had been known to take risks when necessary. Both fearlessly faced challenges head-on when they had to. Yet, the risk of not going back to work and pursuing an artsy uncertain dream was cringe-worthy for both of them. It was way too risky. My mom sighed and waved away my argument, knowing as stubborn as I was, there was no way she'd be able to talk me out of it. She didn't fear my potential success. She feared my possible failure. It seemed inevitable to her. I was okay with failing because I'd rather fail than not try at all. Failure became my teacher.

Despite the warnings, the naysayers and the downright negative comments, I continued to move forward. I put in the same hours writing and publishing books as I did as full-time job corporate employee. I would stop around five or six pm to be available to my family. I worked overtime, sometimes well into the night. I worked weekends and holidays even though none of what I was doing felt like work. I loved every minute of it. Hours sped by, but the passage of time didn't register.

I wrote for hours every weekday. Then, I'd switch gears to handle some kind of business or do research to find out anything else I needed to know to make this project a success. Aspicomm Media was the name of my first company. I registered it with the state department and received my business documents. After that, I applied for a tax ID making Aspicomm Media official. Hours and hours were spent researching every aspect of the business so I could be sure to execute my duties precisely. My bookshelf became filled with books and guides on publishing, running businesses, and marketing. The internet helped to fill other gaps. I wrote in solitude, so I used the internet to find out about and connect with the writing and publishing communities.

Social media wasn't prevalent back then. It didn't even exist. I found much of what I needed to connect with publishers and writers through books, industry magazines, and looking people up on their websites or the sites of major publishers. I found out about literary events happening in my area and around the country and began attending as many as I could afford.

When I completed my manuscripts I turned them over to Susan, who worked for weeks editing them. In the meantime, I reached out to a friend and former co-worker whom I worked with in a previous marketing position. Brian was an amazing graphic artist that created compelling images that I believed seamlessly married content with design. I gave Brian a synopsis of my books, and we discussed options for covers. Brian had never designed a book cover before, but I was confident that he could do a great job. I sent him samples of covers from other authors who wrote in the same genre. Using those as a guide, we worked together to create book covers that fit the vision I'd imagined.

With the editing and cover design underway, I researched book printers. Amazon wasn't around then. I had to find printers through directories. I visited their websites. I contacted three and received quotes and book samples in the mail so I could check the quality. It was important that my books looked just as good as the ones on the shelves at the bookstore. I selected a company out of Ann Arbor, Michigan, based on the quality of the samples they'd mailed to me. I taught myself how to publish books by reading books about getting published, taking workshops on publishing, and speaking with the authors that I'd been developing relationships with.

There was so much to learn about writing, editing, design, layout, business practices, distribution channels, marketing, and promotions. I kept my head in the research and spoke to as many people in the various sectors of the industry as possible. I traveled to conferences, book fairs, festivals, and other events. I'd begun to build a community of other writers on their journeys to become published authors. We'd band together and talk shop, meet up at events, and share any and everything we learned.

I remember when I received my first book galley—a sample of what the book would look like without the official cover. I reviewed the galley and gave the printer the okay. Several more weeks passed, and a large truck pulled up in front of my house one day and unloaded thousands of copies of my book on pallets.

Even as an author, it's almost impossible to describe the feeling of having my thoughts, ideas, and characters show up at my home in the form of a tangible book. There is something truly incredible about seeing something abstract manifest before you in a physical way. Once the books were placed in my garage, I snatched a box and opened it. I pulled out a copy and stared at it. I had a book—an actual completed novel. The title, *Mountain High Valley Low,* was a perfect summation for both the storyline and all that I had gone through in the past year to get to the point where I could hold the book. I turned the book over and over in my hand. I flipped through the pages, smelled the paper, and then ran my fingers over the words—my words. I had done it.

First, I called my husband to let him know that the books had arrived. He cheered for me over the phone. Next, I grabbed a copy and drove to my mother's house. She knew the work I'd been putting in. When I arrived, she was in the kitchen, being the amazing cook she was. That's where she spent most of her time. I dragged her from the kitchen to the living room and made her sit down. I placed the book in her hand. Holding the book, she looked up at me—her mouth agape. She gasped and looked back down at the book. She ran her hand across the cover, flipped through the pages, just like I had as if to confirm that it was real. She opened the pages, ran her fingers over the words. When she finally looked back up at me there were tears in her eyes. Quietly she said, "You did it."

Up to this point, everything about pursuing my passion was indulgent. Even the bad days didn't seem bad. Writing and immersing myself into the fulfillment of my dream felt amazing. I'd found my tribe in the company of writers, avid readers, and the publishing community-at-large. I took writing classes, attempting to hone my skills and become better. I was a writer —a real writer with books with my name scrawled across the cover and a gaggle of other writers to talk shop with. Just letting the words 'writer' and 'author' roll off my tongue felt intoxicating. I was living my dream.

Despite the sacrifices I made and the struggle to live a severely down-scaled version of my life, I was never happier. Sharing my gift with my readers and writing community made sense. It felt right. I hadn't thought about how writing would integrate itself into other areas of my life. I didn't understand the impact that my writing would have on anyone else besides my husband or me until a few distinct and pivotal moments happened on my journey. These were the first of many other significant moments and experiences that led me to realize that my writing wasn't just about me.

The first experiences were simple ones. I'd get emails from readers about how much they enjoyed my stories, how my books offered an escape, or a sense of hope. Some mentioned how they could see themselves in my characters, which was something they were never able to do before and spoke of how validating that felt for them. Aspiring writers who were just short of completing their first novels wrote to me about how I had inspired them to embark on their journeys to become a published author. These experiences touched me and fueled my desire to write more. Even though I'd been moved by some books I read, I hadn't considered how my books might move a reader to laughter or tears. Up until then, I simply wanted at least one person to read and like my book.

One day I received a call from a woman who worked with youth programs for the City of New York. She had become familiar with my books and asked if I would come to talk to the girls in one of her programs. This particular group of girls consisted of young runaways and pregnant teens housed together in a group home in the Bronx, NY. They had never met an author, especially a black one. Since I had always gotten along well with young people and even taught kids and teens as a Sunday school teacher, I gladly accepted the opportunity to visit.

This one visit led to me doing a six-week writing workshop with these girls that began with teaching them about the therapeutic practice of journaling. At first several of the girls in the small group appeared shy and refused to open up. Some seemed downright uninterested or bothered by my presence when I showed up each week. But then something magical happened. At least it was magical to me.

I kept showing up, and the most resistant young lady began to open up to me. I recognized that as trust. Life for her had been extremely difficult, and there weren't many people left that she trusted. Not only did she trust me, but she trusted me with her words and her experiences, and she made them plain on paper. She became vulnerable and bold all at the same time, and the atmosphere changed. I became their mentor, their confidant. We became a sisterhood in which I had the pleasure of helping them navigate through their experiences in life. We talked books, created simple and intricate plots, made up characters together and put them in precarious situations, then imagined how they could wiggle out of them. The stories we created were funny, moving, serious, sad, silly, and ridiculous. We wove our way through real-life stories and intertwined them with made-up ones. I was able to do all of this using my talent, my gift, through one of the things I loved the most —words!

Working with those girls helped me realize another passion that was tied to my purpose, working with youth, especially disadvantaged young people. I spoke to God in prayer saying, "If this is what you want me to do (write and work with youth), show me how to do them together."

In these experiences, writing transcended beyond something I was passionate about. It blossomed into something outside of me, something larger than me that had little to do with me. It had much more to do with those whose lives I intersected with. My passion for writing led me to my purpose. It's one thing to write. It is an entirely different thing to know *why* I write.

Writing and working with young people lead to encounters with the most interesting people and the journey took me down unexpected paths. One person or experience inevitably led to another. People shared how they were impacted by a book or simple conversation we may have had. More and more, I realized I was being led to people on purpose. Either their lives would be changed in some way, or mine would. Through writing, I was able to help at-risk youth find direction or express themselves, navigate pain through words, and become free.

After this, I worked with another group of young ladies at a facility in Brooklyn, a placement home for girls who had been released from jail but were not able to return home just yet. On one particular day I arrived at the facility and checked in. From the moment I entered the secured building, I could feel the tension in the atmosphere. Something had happened. Something bad. The girls usually dispersed themselves around the room where we normally held our writing workshops and when I arrived they would gather so we could start our sessions. This day, no one moved. They were angry. It was apparent that some of them had been crying.

I put my lesson plan aside to give them an opportunity to voice how they were feeling. A few just sucked their teeth. After a bit more prodding, some opened up to express how upset they were at an incident that ultimately impacted all of them negatively. One responded as if she had lost all hope. After listening, I told them we wouldn't be doing the activity I had planned for today. Instead, I wanted them to write about how they were feeling so they could work through those thoughts and emotions. I gave them a simple writing prompt, telling them to write whatever they wanted using the phrase, "Tomorrow Looks Like." I also told them they weren't required to hand in what they decided to write. I simply wanted them to get out what they were feeling.

I handed out paper and pencils. Some girls wrote nothing. I was used to that. Those girls ranged from thirteen to seventeen and had emerged from some of life's most challenging situations, including spending time in juvenile detention centers. Most had experienced more hardships and heartaches than many adults. Large amounts of time spent away from the classroom made them feel insecure about their ability to write well. Our mantra became, "It's not how you say it. It's what you have to say." So when they didn't write, I didn't push them. Eventually, they all became comfortable expressing themselves despite imperfect grammar.

Others wrote poems, and a few simply ranted about that day. One young lady expressed that for her, tomorrow would look the same as always. She'd wake up in that facility again and again, without her family, frustrated, angry, and alone. As a group, we talked through her feelings, calming her down.

One particular girl, who I will call Ally, always refused to put pen to paper. She engaged in the discussion, but never actually wrote anything. She was one of the girls who looked like they'd been crying before I arrived. Today, Ally wrote. She wrote pages upon pages, chronicling the horrors of that day along with her feelings, and frustrations. It was as if a dam had burst and everything in her came pouring out on paper—every hurtful, painful thing she'd ever experienced in her young life. Ally wrote until she couldn't write anymore. Then we talked a bit. I left that day feeling like I'd made very little progress with the girls. I wondered if I had helped any of them at all. I felt bad that I was able to leave and go home to my family, but they had to stay there for weeks or months. I hoped that the little bit of writing that many of them did helped to work off some of the exasperation they felt. I hoped the next session would be better.

I returned the following week to a surprise. Ally had not only continued to write in her journal that evening, but she wrote every single day since. At our next session she was excited to show me everything she had written in the new composition notebook one of the counselors had given her. Not only had Ally worked through her emotions from that day, she had also begun to deal with the very situation that put her in the juvenile detention center in the first place. She freed herself through those words. Ally told me she didn't like writing, but that day changed everything and taught her another way to deal with the things that life threw at her.

Ally had beautifully written her story in prose, poetry, and lyrics that she sometimes performed for the girls and me. Her writing was intriguing and rich in figurative language and symbolism. It was a joy for me to show her all the great writing techniques she had used, something she thought she was incapable of doing. By the time our weekly sessions came to a close, Ally was in tears. She didn't want them to end. She had filled several notebooks with her words. The counselors spoke of the changes they saw in her. I encouraged her to continue to write, to tell her story and work through her feelings. She promised she would because it had changed her life. I knew this experience was purpose-driven. It was ordained. I was to use my gift and passion to help this young woman overcome. It wasn't about me at all. It was all about them. It was all about purpose. I don't take credit for Ally's change. I'm grateful that my passion and I were able to be used as an instrument to help impact Ally's life.

I write to uplift, entertain, and free people. I provide escapes, restore hope, and touch hearts by humanizing experiences. I write to give permission, to validate, and to move people. I write to inspire and to help people see themselves. I write to teach and nourish the seedlings of budding writers. I write because God uses my tiny little slice of life to touch people and change lives. My writing is not just to indulge me, but to fulfill a purpose. It was connected all along. No longer is passion the only reason I write. My *why*, my purpose is why I write.

Like my writing, your passion is designed to lead you to your purpose. While passion is personally fulfilling and indulgent, living out your purpose is about the lives you impact through your passion. It's not about you. It's about God's work and you being used as a vehicle to get His will done.

Here's another way to consider this. We are not just given gifts, talents, and abilities to be cool. We carry a responsibility to put them to use. If we allow it, God will use our gifts to create a life for us. The natural-born musician that never makes any music or the painter that never picks up a brush will never reach their full potential in life. They will never use those gifts to create anything that adds beauty and substance to the world around them. They will never carve out their rightful space in our existence. They will never inspire the next artist. They will never fulfill their purpose for which they were given their incredible gift. And because of this, they risk missing out on so much that life has to offer them. Here's a big one. If you never use your gift, you will never be able to truly glorify God in all your ways.

Jesus told stories in the Bible that are known as parables. Rich in figurative language, each of these parables is packed with layers of spiritual truths, lessons, and relatable narratives. In The Parable of the Talents (Matthew 25:14-30), Jesus tells a story about a man, a master, who goes on a journey and entrusts several talents to each of his servants. Some versions of the Bible use the term bags of gold instead of talents. Talents, at the time, represented a currency. To one servant, he gave one talent. To another, he gave two talents. To the third, he gave five talents. The master went on his journey and returned to find that the servants he entrusted two and five talents to used their talents to gain more. They were both able to double what they were originally given. However, the servant who had one talent buried his and did nothing with it that would cultivate any kind of gain. What happened? In summation, that talent was taken from him and given to one of the other servants. Why? Because he hid it. He didn't make use of it, which is as bad as wasting or squandering it.

Maybe you've heard the saying, if you don't use something, you'll lose it. Our talents are meant to be used, cultivated, developed, and shared with the world. They can be used to create a living. Think about some of the world's most renowned thinkers, artists, athletes, writers, entrepreneurs, and businesses. They took what they had and produced something more significant with it. In the process, they got better at what they were gifted to do. They touched other lives. You don't have to make history to make an impact. I'm sure you can look at people within your circle and recognize how they are using their gifts to make a living, to impact the lives of others, and so many other things. Can't think of anyone? How about that person who makes the best cakes you've ever tasted? What about that book you read that made a lasting impression? Think about the last person you encountered with the gift of gab that talked you into doing something or buying something you didn't anticipate doing or buying. What about the person that inspires you every time they open their mouth? Guess what? Any example you can think of is evidence that you encountered someone's gift.

The more writers write, the better they get at writing. The more technology developers develop, the more they change the way we live through technology. When we use our gifts, we fine-tune them. The better we get with our gifts, the more we can do with them. The more we do with a gift, the more we increase our potential to impact other people's lives. Think about the amount of time that people who operate in their gifts spend working on getting better.

If you've got a gift, use it. Using our gifts is about so much more than just indulging our abilities. It's not just about us. It's about what we contribute to the world. It's about the lives we touch through the use of our gifts. Think about how things other people in this world created have been helpful to you. Think about that life-changing book or the technology that made life a bit more convenient. What about something someone said that made you look at them, yourself, or the world differently? Someone's obedient use of their talent lies at the core of every epiphany you've ever had. It was hearing something someone said, seeing something someone did, reading something someone wrote, experiencing something someone created. These experiences inspire action, thoughts, and ideas.

Using your gift is not just about you. It is also for those who will look at what you're doing and become inspired enough to believe that they can do it too. Use your gift because it will release possibilities for both you and others. It will be fulfilling. Use your gift to make your mark on the world. Use your gift to inspire someone else to use theirs. Use your gift to create the life you want to live. Use your gift to live out your purpose in life.

And most importantly, use your gift to glorify God. How do you do that? When people come in contact with your gift, and they are thankful for having had that experience, their gratefulness gives God joy. How many times have you been moved by something someone said, did, or created? That joy you experienced by that encounter gives God joy because that's precisely why He gave the person their gift in the first place.

Passion Vs. Purpose

My dreams manifested. I was living my passion out loud. I thought that's what the entire journey was all about. It felt amazing. It was indulgent. I served people, and my passion served me. I'd write and feel good. I'd teach and feel great. I'd serve and feel rewarded. All of it made me feel empowered. Along the way, I learned a valuable lesson that changed my whole perspective of purpose and passion.

I initially mistook my passion for a hobby. I happily spent time engaging in the thing I loved doing, and it felt amazing. I earned money doing it, and that made me feel like anything was possible. Hours passed and I wouldn't notice, nor did I care. I was enjoying myself. Living this way led to the understanding that there was so much more that could be done. There was more to this passionate way of life. Indulging my passion wasn't something to be relegated to my spare time, and most importantly, it wasn't just about me.

Scripture tells us, *"No one lights a lamp and puts it in a place where it will be hidden, or under a bowl. Instead, they put it on its stand, so that those who come in may see the light." Luke 11:33 NIV.* Passion is like this light. It is supposed to shine for all who can see it. It's a living thing that maneuvers through life with us. It grows and deepens. It inspires and connects us to others. It compels us and moves us forward. It possesses a power that has enough force to propel us through challenges and over obstacles.

Passion serves us in several other ways. It fuels our hope, exercises our resilience, powers endurance, and covers the cost of the losses acquired from our sacrifices. It carries out its mission. Yes. Passion has a mission, which is to lead us to our purpose.

While passion serves us, purpose, on the other hand, has almost nothing to do with us. However, it has everything to do with those who are impacted as a result of crossing paths with our passion. Your purpose is the 'higher why' of all you do. It's above you; stronger than you. It's the existential call; the reason for your dream, the fulfillment of your passion's mission. Purpose is the lifeblood of the Dream Journey.

Several profound moments in my life reinforced the differences between passion and purpose for me. These instances helped me to understand what I call the "higher why."

I took my background in marketing, my proficiency in delivering compelling presentations, and my joy of teaching and created workshops around finding and indulging one's passion.

My first workshop was called Passion, Platform, Profits. It was all about finding ways to profit from one's passion. I was onto something, but hadn't fully realized it. I was teaching people how to make a few dollars off their passions. Purpose wasn't part of this class, nor was there anything in it about developing a lifestyle of passion and purpose. Dream journey wasn't even a twinkle in my mind's eyes yet. But people were inspired, and I was happy to motivate them toward some action.

I guided my audiences through strategies for uncovering their passions. I provided activities that made them think and dig deep to figure out what things bought them joy and challenged them to spend more time doing those things. I told them that they would come to know their passions. Signs would include never tiring of those activities and desiring to engage in those things as much as possible. I encouraged them to measure the sense of pleasure they experienced when they were engaged in those things they loved. I had them explore all their proclivities and pay special attention to the things they had natural talents for. They examined what they did well without effort and assessed their skills. I told them if they indulged in the things they thought they were passionate about, and the passing of time didn't matter to them, that was a clue they were operating in their passion. I'm not sure if I ever mentioned the word purpose one time. They practiced indulgence, and for some of them, it changed their lives.

Then I had an epiphany. This thing I was doing—showing people how to indulge their passions and potentially profit from them—didn't just give me joy. These lessons changed people's lives. It was about opening a door in the hearts and minds of people. It was about me being used as an instrument to lead them to their dreams and passions, and ultimately their purpose. God was using me. My purpose was being fulfilled while I indulged my passion. The purpose was even more important because it impacted more lives than just mine. This work wasn't just what I liked to do. It's what I was *supposed* to be doing.

Having talents and passions and dreams is not random. These are not untethered parts of a coincidence. They are all intricately designed to be a significant part of your life. They are to be something that guides you in your living. You are to use them.

CHAPTER 4

$\mathcal{G}$etting Ready

FOR MY TWENTIETH WEDDING ANNIVERSARY, my husband and I decided to renew our vows. We planned a trip to Costa Rica for a destination vow renewal. My sister was determined to be there with us despite not having the extra cash to cover the cost of her trip. But that didn't stop her. Every time the subject came up, she'd insist she was going. We weren't going to leave her behind. She didn't know how, but she was going to be there. One day in an act of sheer faith, my sister pulled out her suitcase and began filling it with items she wanted to take with her on the trip. For the next few months, she sought out bargains to find other things she wanted to take with her, including the dress she would wear to the renewal. At this point, she hadn't booked her vacation package with the travel agent, nor had she secured her flight. She simply didn't have the funds, yet she insisted she'd be there.

Months passed, and then weeks. The time for us to leave drew near. Everyone who planned to travel with us had now paid for their trips in full. We had been planning for over a year. Less than thirty days before our departure another family member had come across extra money and gave my sister the money to cover the full cost of her trip. She grabbed that bag she'd been packing for several months, and just like she said she would, she joined us in Costa Rica.

It's Going to Take Faith

For years I'd marveled at this particular sister's faith. This trip to Costa Rica wasn't the first time I'd witnessed her exercise that unwavering faith of hers. It didn't matter if she couldn't see how something would come together. She took whatever steps she could to make it happen and left the details up to God. She leaned on her faith and trusted that God would make a way, and He often did. Because of her, I call this "Pack Your Bags" kind of faith. She put her faith in action, and her actions often made way for many things in her life to manifest through faith. That's the kind of faith we need when pursuing a dream. The outcome is always uncertain, but you have to move forward as if it was guaranteed.

For this to work, we have to first take our dreams seriously. My sister was serious about everything she had faith in. Far too many people think of dreams as being whimsical, imaginative, unrealistic, or intangible. Some are frightened of what they dream because they seem so vast and impossible. For these reasons, people don't act upon their dreams. They don't believe they are attainable. Millions of people have literally talked themselves out of pursuing their dreams or allowed friends and family members to do the same. Every negative idea associated with dreams is rooted in fear—fear of ridicule, failure, or being considered ridiculous for believing their zany notions were even possible.

On the contrary, dreams are nothing to be afraid of. They are simply ideas, ideas that may seem unusual or far-fetched, but still ideas. They have a purpose, and if given the right energy, they have the potential to manifest into amazing material things or real-life experiences that can change one's life or even the world.

You know every well-known person from history through today became well-known because of an idea—from inventors to artists, advocates, educators, entrepreneurs, architects, and entertainers. Their journeys began with a simple idea they gave energy to and leaned on faith to achieve. Everything around you, from the book in your hand, the chair you're sitting on, the company you work for, tablet, computer, or the phone you surf the internet on started as an idea.

There is power in your ideas and thoughts. They're like seeds. If watered, they can blossom into incredibly fruitful concepts, materials, inventions, etc. from the most straightforward item to complex, brilliant strategies. Microsoft, Apple, Ford, Amazon are all companies that began in a single person's mind, yet they revolutionized the way we live. What if Bill Gates, Steve Jobs, Henry Ford, and Jeff Bezos had kept their ideas to themselves?

We can be confident that these individuals shared their ideas with people and were probably called ridiculous or told they were impossible to achieve. I'm sure they even attempted to talk themselves out of their ideas or thoughts. They must have been afraid. I believe they may have even procrastinated a bit when it came to acting on these ideas. But these nagging thoughts and ideas just wouldn't go away. They returned to them day after day, week after week, month after month, and even year after year until they could no longer ignore them. Eventually, it didn't matter who thought their ideas were crazy. Undoubtedly

IBM inspired the work of Microsoft and Apple. And without the work of these two major entities, there wouldn't have been a need for the internet. And without the internet, would there be no Amazon. The manifestation of IBM's ideas created a platform for Microsoft and Apple, which gave way to the World Wide Web and created a space for companies like Amazon to exist. Now, what if the founder of IBM never acted on his original idea, which at the time probably seemed a bit unrealistic?

Most people can't visualize their ideas until they materialize into something understandable or physical. That's because it's hard for people to imagine something that never existed before. Despite how nutty their ideas seemed, they changed life as we knew it. Imagine living without computers, cell phones, cars, and the ability to go online and order almost anything you could need. These individuals are just a few examples of those who were determined enough to see their ideas materialize. They failed along the way, but eventually succeeded in bringing their ideas to life. They didn't quit on their dream.

People quit on their dreams every minute of every day. But there are a select few that don't. That won't—that simply can't. Their dreams—these thoughts or ideas—cling, refusing to accept abandonment. Sooner or later, the dream wins. These people are real dreamers. They harbor ideas that just won't die. Eventually, they embrace their dreams, put plans into action, work those plans, and persevere toward success. The world needs these dreams. They serve a purpose, fill gaps, change lives. This world requires its dreamers to dream and then plan, act, and execute. And the dreamer needs faith.

Inside your mind there's an idea unlike any. This idea has been with you for a while. It started as a seed and now begs to be nurtured. It won't be ignored. Perhaps you're stuck on the planning part or you're not sure how to act on your dream. Maybe execution is your issue. You might be ready to forge forward, but need a push or some kind of confirmation.

I urge you to indulge that dream, that thought, that idea. Spend time with it. Feed it. Nurture it. Create a plan, act, and execute. Allow your faith to fill all the gaps you can't seem to fill. You'll meet some failure along the way. Failure is your teacher—educating you on the right and wrong way to go about something. Failure serves as your guide as much as inspiration does. I promise you that once you set out on your journey to see your dream come to fruition, you'll be amazed at what unfolds when your imagination meets the reality it fostered. Whether it manifests into a product, concept, or experience, the result is likely to blow your mind. It will show up exceedingly more abundant than what you thought or imagined.

Jeff Bezos didn't know he would become the world's largest online retailer when he got the idea to start selling books out of his garage. The "Steves," Steve Jobs and Steve Wozniak of Apple, hadn't imagined becoming one of the globe's most cutting-edge technology brands when they put those first fifty computers together and sold them to local retailers. Bill Gates set out to develop new software for computers, not a technology empire. With limited formal education, Henry Ford left a job to indulge his 'crazy' idea of creating a motor car. They didn't set out to develop world-renowned companies or revolutionize the way society operated. They intended to act on simple ideas—ideas that became Amazon, Apple, Microsoft, and Ford Motor Company.

You, too, have these incredible seedlings of thoughts and ideas inside you. What is the difference between you, these men, and the countless other people who we've come to know because they had an idea? People like Oprah Winfrey, Estee Lauder, Martin Luther King, Walt Disney, JK Rowling, Madam CJ Walker, Mark Zuckerberg, and so many more. If you're a dreamer, there's no difference between you and these trailblazers. It doesn't matter how big or small your idea is. It doesn't matter if your dream impacts a community or the world at large. What matters is that it is imperative for your dream to come to fruition. This world is holding a space for the ideas that will go through you. You're already equipped for the manifestation of your dreams through your gifts and talents. You just need to allow your ideas to flourish and then cultivate them. What matters even more is that you're a dreamer, and you cannot and will not quit your dream. Your purpose is embedded in your dream. For your dream to be fulfilled, you have to act on it whether you see it as possible or not. Act as though it is already in the works.

For your dreams to manifest, you must exercise your faith. Faith is the bridge between dreaming and living a life inspired by your dreams. You may not be able to see the fullness of what you envision, nor will you know everything you need to know to embark on your dream journey, but you can't let that stop you. Faith can open the door of possibilities that you can't see. *Now faith is the substance of things hoped for, the evidence of things not seen. (Hebrews 11:1 NKJV).* This Word of God puts it all into perspective. No journey or idea started without a measure of faith. Something inside of each person who accomplished something new operated on faith. When you're beginning, it's impossible to know how things will go, but activate your faith so that you can one day find out. Activating your faith means putting your faith into action. Having faith is one thing, but putting your faith into action is a whole different thing. Active faith is what you need for this journey. For years, I credited myself for having faith, but I hadn't put that faith into action.

Stacey Ciceron is my accountability partner. We will talk more about accountability in the coming chapters. She was also my fabulous hairstylist whose childhood dream was to be a beautician. Starting as a stylist, Stacey went on to become a celebrity stylist, ambassador for top beauty brands, an educator, consultant, coach, and influencer. When she first started playing in her friend's hair as a young aspiring hairdresser, she hadn't anticipated carving such an accomplished path in the beauty industry. When she enrolled in beauty school, the thought of styling top models during fashion week in New York, Miami, Paris, or Milan hadn't crossed her mind. But she wasn't scared to dream. She also made room for faith to push her to fill in the gaps between what she could imagine as possible.

One particular day after styling my hair, Stacey placed me under the dryer and in the usual fashion, plopped down next to me to chat. We talked about everything under the sun, but our conversations always circled back to our dreams and the things we accomplished. This particular day, like many others, I mentioned to her how I wanted to make it as an author. At that point, I had self-published a few books but dreamed of being an author with a book deal at a major publishing house and a large following of readers. That day, Stacey challenged me and asked what I needed to do in the next thirty days to make that happen. I was both taken aback and excited by that question. Her inquiry required that I be intentional. Follow-up questions required that I imagine all the possibilities and, most importantly, that I have faith and act on it.

That day we both made plans to pursue our dreams and act on our faith. We planned out what we could do in our power and strength. We planned based on what we knew we could do, and then we prepared for stronger possibilities even though we didn't know how we could accomplish them. We relied on faith to fill the gap. We acted on them with a sense of expectation as if all of our plans were guaranteed to manifest, despite some of them being outside of our power to make it happen. We made the leap, activated our faith, and relied on the combination of planning and active faith to take us to new levels. That's how we injected our confidence into the dream—with action and expectations.

We may have been crazy, but we expected our plans to work. That expectation, along with planning, was our faith in action.

Thirty days later, we were to check in with each other and see what progress we'd made. By the time we met, both of us had so much to report. I had reached out to authors who had achieved the things I was trying to achieve. I emailed potential agents and created goals for upcoming publishing events. I prayed, planned, worked, and focused. That time became a turning point in my career as an author. Since then, I have secured an agent, been offered multiple publishing deals, and experienced some of the most mind-blowing experiences of my writing career.

I was asked to join a group of writers on a mission trip to a small, impoverished village in Ghana, Africa, to help build a library, assist with school improvements, develop literacy programs, and work on a scholarship program to help pay for young people to attend school. That trip turned into the beginning of a nonprofit organization with a mission to provide innovative literacy programs and scholarships to students for the next several years. I never imagined my writing would take me there. But that's what acting on faith will do to your dreams, open doors for you that you couldn't have imagined. This is just one of the incredible experiences I've had the privilege to engage in as a result of really acting on my dreams and my faith.

Like my sister packing her bags, think about what steps you can take to act on your faith, and make your dreams a reality. Create your plan. Visualize your outcome. Set some goals. Act on faith and set out on your journey with an expectation of achieving your dreams.

GET Your Mind Right

Understanding that the pursuit of your dreams is a journey is a vital starting point. We also know that figuring out where you are in the process is critical. The lives you will impact are crucial. However, another critical component of a successful dream journey is making sure you are mentally ready. The right mindset can make or break your journey, so it's imperative to get your mind right before your dreams can truly take off.

God began to deal with me in my dreams. He taught me lessons, showed me where I needed to grow, helped me build my confidence, and revealed areas in my life that I needed to fix. At first, these dreams boggled me. Some made me nervous because I didn't understand them. Some were scary. Some were downright hilarious, like when I was running through the streets of New York City with no pants on. And yes, no under-garments either. I'll explain more about that soon. But the more I had these dreams, the more I learned how to deal with them and realized what I was supposed to get from them. I prayed and reached out to people I knew could pray for me and under-stand my dreams.

I was in my thirties when I discovered that writing was my passion. I decided I wanted to spend more time writing and developing my talent. I published my first book and started to gain some real recognition. I loved it. It was what I had asked for. But I also realized that I wasn't really comfortable with the attention I gained. When I released my second book, I had a book release event hosted by a magazine that was growing in popularity at the time. It was amazing. Press from the magazine snapped pictures all over the place. They'd caught me as I came in and captured shots of me with friends from the publishing industry and guests. My family and friends were all in atten-dance. Other authors whom I'd met along the way were there as well.

That night, I felt like I'd made it. However, as happy as I was, I became increasingly uncomfortable as the event went on. Though I kept a smile on my face, I started feeling overwhelmed by all the attention. After a while, I no longer wanted to take pictures. Sincere accolades from guests that I invited seemed like too much. I just wanted to go home. This reaction continued through several other events. I was okay at home while working on my books, but being out in the spotlight left much to be desired. I had these big dreams and wanted to be successful, but as soon as the spotlight shined my way, I wanted someone to turn it off so I could crawl under a boulder somewhere. I wasn't camera shy, so that wasn't it. I just couldn't take the feeling of too many people fawning over me. But the more I pursued my dream of writing and speaking, the more unavoidable the spotlight became. What was wrong with me? I had developed a fan base that I both wanted and couldn't stand.

More dreams came like the one where I was running half-naked. I was walking with a friend one evening on a busy street in New York City. I happened to look down and realized I was naked from the waist down. How had this happened? Here I was in the middle of a crowded city block with no underwear, no pants, not a single article of clothing below my shirt, not even shoes. My heart dropped. I grabbed my friend's hand. "Oh, My God! I'm half-naked!"

Until that point, she hadn't even noticed. I took off running. Where was I going? Who knew? I just had to get off those streets. I ran through alleys and the backs of busy restaurants looking for a place I could take cover. I passed through patrons enjoying meals alfresco on city blocks and saw my eldest sister sitting down having dinner. This sister is like our mother. She's always concerned about our well-being, and even she didn't notice. I heard her ask the person she was dining with, "Why is Renee running like that?"

My friend and I ran toward some brownstones and I recognized an old friend from the neighborhood where I grew up. He told me to come inside, and he'd help me. It was the weirdest dream I'd ever had—up to that point. For days I wondered what it was about. I prayed, Googled 'naked in dreams,' and called people to pray for me and to find out what this meant. I was told that I was uncomfortable with exposure, and the fact that no one else in the dream appeared to be alarmed by my 'nakedness' meant I was the only one who had a problem with it. People expected me to have this exposure—even my family members. That was eye-opening. I vowed to work on that.

Meanwhile, my writing career continued to take off. I'd worked hard at being the best writer I could be. I was asked to be part of a panel of authors speaking at an event. Right in the middle of the session I stopped, looked from one side to the other, and sighed. I sat between two well-known, award-winning, trailblazing romance writers and couldn't believe that I had been chosen to sit amongst them. It felt great to be considered on their level, but it also made me anxious. I wondered if I belonged on that stage beside them.

I had another naked dream. This time I was completely naked, sitting on an airplane. Again, no one seemed to notice. The stewardesses and fellow passengers who all happened to be fully dressed paid me no mind. I sat strapped in my chair as naked as the day I was born, sipping on water and laughing at the fact that no one noticed. To everyone around me, things seemed perfectly normal. When I exited the plane I walked through the airport just as naked, shaking my head at how I was being ignored. I didn't receive curious stares, scowls, raised brows, nothing! No one was fazed. At this point I began to care less and less about the fact that I wasn't wearing any clothes. And the most interesting part was that somehow, even in the dream, I was keenly aware of how the dream compared to my first dream where I was only half-naked.

As the dream continued, I strolled through a pristine white airport and all of a sudden I spotted the entertainer, Steve Harvey. People surrounded him on all sides. I assumed they were part of his entourage. As we approach one another he looked over, pointed, and said, "I see you." He let out his infamous big laugh and continued his confident stride. Then he disappeared into thin air. I woke up laughing hysterically.

Finally, it was coming together for me. I called the same people and gave them an update on my latest dream. Before I spoke to them, I knew some of what they were going to say. The message had already begun to settle in my spirit. Here it was:

The more successful I was becoming, the more exposure I gained. At first, it made me uncomfortable. My exposure or being in the spotlight wasn't a surprise to anyone. In fact, others expected me to be successful, which is why my being fully exposed wasn't out of place for them. It was a natural part of my journey. I was the only one who had a problem with it. This dream confirmed that while I was still uncomfortable with exposure, I was getting better at handling it. To sum this up, I had made progress, but still had work to do with being comfortable with my success. I needed a mindset shift.

God showed me something about myself. My mindset of not being comfortable with what I had asked for blocked what I desired. I was hindering my success, and unless I dealt with my attitude toward success, I couldn't access the fullness of it.

I spent time trying to figure out what my problem was. I realized that I wanted to be successful but didn't believe it was possible. Therefore, the idea of success simply made me uncomfortable. The exposure came with success, and I had to work on thinking I was not only capable, but that I was worthy. I also felt guilty for desiring to be successful. As confident as I appeared to be on the outside, my mindset presented a different reality. I had to rewire my belief system.

I worked to get rid of those negative thoughts and replaced them with new truths that reinforced that I was worthy of success and that God Himself wanted me to be successful. To truly embrace success, opportunities, and even our dreams, we have to believe that it's possible. I also had to learn that it was God's will for me to prosper.

I knew my talent had come from God. I also knew that my passion was tied to my purpose and that my purpose was to glorify God with my gifts. Yet, I didn't believe it was okay to dream big and prosper, and that was a major monkey wrench in my ability to fully embrace my journey. I was uncertain about whether it was okay to desire big things, and I didn't want God to be upset with me for not having my priorities in order.

Your mindset is your belief system. If your belief system about yourself is flawed, it will always be in the way of your progress. Since pleasing God is what I desired the most, I started with the Bible. I needed to make sure it was okay to pursue my dreams and enjoy the amazing lifestyle that it was capable of offering without feeling guilty about it. I had to toss out my belief that I shouldn't desire abundance and prosperity, and that's what I believed pursuing my dreams would bring— abundant life and prosperity.

In the word of God, I discovered truths that became part of my new belief systems. Through the Word, I developed a new mindset around dreams, desires, abundance, and prosperity. Scriptures like *"The blessings of the Lord makes one rich and he adds no sorrow with it,"* Proverbs *10:22, NKJV* and *"The thief does not come except to steal, and to kill and to destroy. I have come that they may have life and that they may have it more abundantly,"* John *10:10, NKJV.* Other scriptures like Ephesians 3:20 NKJV, *"Now unto Him who can do exceedingly abundantly above all that we ask or think according to the power that works in us,"* and Jeremiah 29:11, *"For I know the thoughts that I think toward you, says the Lord, thoughts of peace and not of evil to give you a future and a hope,"* and so many more helped me reshape my mindset.

My new truths became my new belief system. I had altered my mindset. It didn't happen overnight. Day after day, I reminded myself that I was worthy of success, that it was okay to be successful, and through scripture, I developed confidence that God desired for us to be successful. I read every part of the Bible that supported this fact until I believed it for myself in my heart.

Get your mind right and ready for the journey. You are enough. You do deserve this. You do belong. You were made to do this. There's a seat at the table waiting just for you. You can embrace your dreams fully, and all that is possible because of them. You have your gifts, your plans, your faith, and now you have the right mindset to carry with you on the journey. You're ready for God to use you and change your life and the lives of others. Now go!

CHAPTER 5

❧

Be Ready for the Hard Parts

JUST LIKE WITH any trip or journey, it's essential to be prepared for unexpected outcomes. When I travel, I make sure I carry a first aid kit with me in the case of sickness or injury. Items in this kit may include bandages, alcohol wipes, antiseptic sprays, antibiotic ointments, pain relievers, allergy pills, etc. There's no guarantee that I'll need any of these items, but it's essential to have them if a need arises.

No matter how much we prepare for a journey, there will always be times when our fuel runs low, detours are necessary, or the road simply gets bumpy. Because I vow to keep things real, I believe it's just as important to share the aspects of this journey that are not so joyful. These 'bumps in the road' are as important as our wins because, in the end, they shape us and teach us some of our most valuable lessons.

· · ·

Sacrifice Has ROI

To be successful in your dream journey, you must make sacrifices. However, these sacrifices are not ones where you simply lose. Think of these as more of an investment that offers a return later.

Sacrifice is a big part of the dream journey. While I'm not an advocate of putting your entire life on hold to achieve a singular goal, it's necessary to make sacrificial choices for the sake of a more significant gain. This is about making very intentional decisions to achieve your goals. It's as simple as getting your priorities in order. There are things you will avoid doing or refrain from doing to make room for what you want to do. In these situations, your dream is taking precedence. As I mentioned before, your dream journey will be your way of life —your new lifestyle. Developing a lifestyle will require you to make a series of choices that will change the usual course that you've traveled up until now and require you to start on a path that will initially appear uncertain.

In 2004, after my third layoff in three years, I decided to leave corporate America behind for good. It was the scariest and most liberating decision I had ever made in my life. Having children didn't frighten me that much. However, I knew two very important things: 1. Corporate America wasn't as secure as it is perceived to be. 2. Being in corporate America wasn't helping me achieve the life I desired.

I asked myself whether I could get closer to living the life I wanted to live working in marketing, or by charting a new course for my life? I decided to take my chances on charting a new course. This meant I needed to start from the bottom all over again. I was also told I needed to learn a new industry and skills. I had to reinvent myself. I became an entrepreneur and started a business I knew very little about.

I invested in my new company, and at first, I made very little in return. Most of my money had to go right back into the business to help keep it afloat. My household income was cut in half. This meant we had to find creative ways to drastically reduce household expenses to get by. After managing bills, we had only small amounts of money left over for necessary household needs. We had already practiced strict austerity with my previous layoffs, so this wasn't new to me. Not being able to go out to dinner with friends because we just didn't have the extra money was daunting. We went weeks without cable, and this was before smart TVs gave us more options. We stopped taking vacations. We managed every aspect of life with the bare minimum. We lived off little to no disposable income. Living like that was frustrating and challenging. But it wasn't as hard as waking up every day and trekking into a job I hated, and if I had the chance, I would do it all again.

I had found my passion and was determined to live, work, earn, and breathe by it. I boldly told the Lord that I wanted to operate by my gift fully. If writing was what I was gifted to do, I wanted to use writing to earn a living. I wanted my gift to open doors to more opportunities. I remembered a scripture that said, *"Ask, and it will be given to you; seek, and you will find; knock, and it will be opened to you,"* Matthew 7:7 NKJV. So I asked! It took time, but I eventually got there. Through a series of very intentional decisions, I finally made it to a point in life where every dollar I earned came directly from writing or some aspect of working in and around the world of writing. I wrote books and articles and taught writing. I facilitated writing workshops and traveled the world to attend writing and publishing events.

I knew it would take a while to get to the point where I could earn a salary similar to what I had made as a marketing professional. I also knew that if I called it quits on my dream and went back to corporate America, I could probably solve all my money issues. However, I preferred the life that I was living so much more. I was able to earn a steady income and generate additional streams of income by teaching in different environments, writing books, and working as a freelance journalist. I often traveled and met the most interesting people. I was able to enlarge my network and gained new friends in different places. Many times, the costs of my travel were covered by companies producing events around literature. I created my schedule, which allowed me to be home with my children more and be active in their schools during their formative years. I served on the PTA, participated in teacher interviews with my kid's school district, and had the flexibility to take my mother to doctor appointments when her health began to fail.

As a marketing professional, I spent an hour and a half commuting every morning from the suburbs to New York City or New Jersey. I worked more than 50 hours each week and traveled another hour and a half back home every night. By the time I got home to my family, I had about two hours to cook, eat, check homework, spend a few moments with my kids, chat with my husband about his busy day, put the kids to bed, and crash just to get up and start all over again the next day.

Now don't get me wrong. For a while, I thrived on that lifestyle. But I decided I no longer wanted to live that way. If I spent countless hours working so hard, I wanted to do it indulging in my passion. If I could put in long hours for someone else's company, I could put in long hours for me. I enjoyed the flexibility my new lifestyle offered. After a while, I no longer cared if I couldn't go out to dinner often. It didn't matter that I had to simplify my life down to bare bones. I was happier, more productive, and living a much more exciting life where I got up every single day and engaged in the things I loved doing. The sacrifice was a tradeoff. Instead of earning a high salary, I made less and got more out of life.

In the midst of that, I discovered I had another passion. I was often asked if I would visit a school or group of young people in various programs or with community-based organizations. I always said yes, and one day realized that I had a love for working with children. That gave me another thing to ask of God. "Lord. Now I want opportunities that will allow me to write, teach writing, and work with kids more consistently, and I want to get paid to do it." And that's just what happened.

It started with the group of teen moms in the Bronx. Since then, I have worked with young people in every environment, from public schools to prisons and community-based organizations. Even now, as I write this book, I run a nonprofit organization that works to provide comprehensive programs for girls to help bridge learning and skills gaps, provide a safe mentoring space, and advocate for their rights. When I'm not working with the organization, I'm writing books, traveling, speaking, teaching, and facilitating workshops on writing and publishing.

I desire to live a life where I get up every day and do what I love, but it is impossible to achieve without sacrifice. There were many days when I wanted to just give up. At times, I did grow tired of living on a shoe-string budget but I didn't give up.

During my pursuit to find an agent to represent me as an author, I received one rejection letter after the other until a publisher finally decided they wanted to offer me a publishing contract. I'm still experiencing my share of ups and downs, but that's how life goes, whether you are living your dream journey or not. The journey ebbs and flows. There are still good and bad days, but there's nothing compared to the joy of continually operating in your gifts and doing what you love.

Giving Up is Not an Option

Speaking of giving up, I had to commit to the idea that giving up was not an option. It wasn't an easy concept to stick to at the time, but it helped me stay grounded. When my days got rough, or checks got low, I'd contemplate going back to corporate America. By then, even my husband was convinced that going back to something I didn't love wouldn't make sense.

He'd remind me that no matter what I did, there were going to be good days and bad days. A bad day doing what you love is better than any good day doing something you don't love. I love my new life. What could make me think of giving it up? Oh! Let me count the things.

There were so many times that I seriously thought about quitting my dream, like when bills piled up, when rejection letters filled my inbox, or when a project didn't turn out as successfully as I had imagined. All these situations challenged my will, my worth, and my desire to continue on the path I had chosen. Many of them had me doubting if I made the right decision. I learned a valuable lesson in this. It's something I mentioned before. Even if you're working in your dream, every day won't be a 'good day,' but it's still so much better than your worst day doing what you don't love.

I recall one particular situation when I received a bad review on one of my books. It was my very first and only unfavorable review. At that time I'd written and published several books and was eventually picked up by a small press. This book had just come out days before, and I did the ridiculous, novel thing of running to check my reviews every five minutes. One of the first reviews posted for this book was horrible. As I read the review, my eyes grew wide and my jaw dropped. The reader hadn't even finished the book, but saw fit to tell other people not to bother buying it. My heart stopped and then broke. I felt like she was talking to me personally. I was hurt and insulted, and then I did the craziest thing. I questioned my ability, my gift, my talent. I had no idea who this person was. She wasn't someone from the publishing industry who could make or break my writing career. Yet, I felt like it was all over for me. She was a reader. Readers are vital to me and I value their opinion. That's all that mattered at that moment—that one reader's opinion, which she audaciously expressed.

After I gathered the pieces of myself that had fallen apart as I read the review, I continued questioning myself. I even wondered why my editor hadn't told me the book was terrible. I had friends who read it and they failed to tell me that I wrote a complete bomb.

I called one of my closest friends, who was also an author. When she picked up the phone I blurted out all the details of that horrible book review. I even asked her about her opinion of my writing. She remained silent as I ranted and raved. That was it. I wasn't writing another book. When I finally took a breath, my friend laughed. She laughed at me. I was livid at first, but then curiosity replaced the anger. What was so funny? Finally, she asked, "Renee, is this your first bad review?" That stopped me in my tracks. It was my first bad review, but I couldn't see how that mattered. Now, this friend has been quite successful in her writing career and wrote for several publishers simultaneously. She has a sizable following. She told me to look at her books and check out her reviews, and then look at others. She named a few authors that we both loved and believed that their writing was excellent, prolific. Then she said, 'Girl, we all get a few bad reviews. It isn't the end of the world." She talked me out of quitting the writing game. That book ended up being one of the best-reviewed books out of most that I had written. It was even nominated for several literary awards, and I was ready to give it all up for one bad review. Of course, I went on to continue writing. One of the books I wrote after that was optioned for film.

Now, what if I had let my emotions get the best of me and stopped writing because one person said they didn't like the book? I would have missed out on all the amazing accomplishments after that. Quitting made sense to me at that moment. Looking back at that, I realized the situation made me a stronger writer.

This dream came with just as many ups and downs as the life I had walked away from. But when I worked for corporations, I didn't consider quitting at the end of a hard day. Why was I considering leaving when something didn't go right while I was operating in my dream? I made the very intentional decision to react to my dream, the same way I did to my jobs in the corporate world, shake it off and get back in the game.

FIGURE OUT WHAT Fear is Telling You

Fear is a scary monster if you allow it to be. Ever notice how your shadow can appear much larger than your actual size? Like fear, it seems so much bigger than it really is. Anxiety is often all bark and no bite.

However, fear is real and legitimate and frightening. We feel it, taste it and see it whether it's our hearts pumping fast, an instant dry mouth, or hives breaking out on our skin. Worst of all, fear can be paralyzing. Instead of trying to be fearless, we should learn how to navigate fear. Fear isn't all bad.

Fear has stopped dreams in their tracks and caused them to dry up and die. I believe the reason for this is because we've chosen to give fear too much power. If you're interested in successfully walking out this journey, it's essential to take that power back. Instead of thinking of fear as this substantial paralyzing monster, I like to think of it as an alert system. If a fire alarm goes off, we try to ensure our safety, but we also find out what made it go off in the first place. When fear arises, the idea is not to just stop everything and give it all up. Instead, we need to address it, deal with it, and explore what's caused it. There's often valuable information to be learned when we examine fear.

When I first told my mother I had a passion for writing and wanted to pursue that full time, she thought I was crazy. My mother tried everything she could to talk me out of it, including implying that my desire made no sense. She told me I'd better find another job. Initially, I was upset by her response. I wanted her support. I questioned why she didn't believe in me—writing made me happy. Why didn't she want me to be satisfied? Eventually, I realized that she was discouraging me because she thought she was helping me. Her actions rose out of her fear. Fear that I would fail. Fear that I wouldn't be able to make a decent living. Fear of me forging ahead into unchartered territory. She hadn't personally known any writers or had exposure to all the people who lived successful lifestyles as writers. It wasn't that she didn't want to see me happy. She wanted the best for me. However, out of love, she tried to save me from myself and the crazy ideas I always seemed to have.

Honestly, I shared some of her fears, but I couldn't allow them to stop me from trying. Her fear had the opposite effect on me. Instead of canceling my plans to become a writer, I forged ahead, determined to prove her and any other naysayers wrong. In that scenario and so many others, I began learning how to walk with my fear instead of allowing it to stop me in my tracks.

Fear became my alert system. When fear arises, I figure out where it's coming from and what it's trying to tell me. Examining my fears has exposed some of the insecurities I harbored. I contemplated giving up my writing dream after one bad review. It wasn't because of that reader. I was fearful of rejection. I felt rejected as a writer and never wanted to feel that again. If I didn't write another book, I would never be rejected by a reader ever again. I was an insecure writer at that time. Knowing that my insecurities were at the root of that fear, I focused on building my skills and confidence as a writer.

When we feel fearful, we need to understand what's causing the fear and address that thing. What we should never do is allow it to stunt our progress or growth. My worries have shed light on my lack of confidence, fear of failure, and even my concern about what people will think of me. How many times has your fear been tied to what other people will think or say?

I often speak at events, and on occasion, I've been fearful of going on stage to deliver speeches before people. I'm not shy, so I realized that the root of that fear wasn't stage fright. Instead, fear of getting up before audiences arises when I am not fully prepared. The source of that fear is due to my lack of preparation. I didn't want to go on stage and look like a fool. As a result, I changed my behavior to make sure I was always adequately prepared, and that particular fear never raised its scary head again. In that situation, fear helped me grow.

The worst thing about allowing fear to paralyze you is that it robs you of memorable experiences, progress, and growth. Don't give it that much power. Feel it, figure it out, and forge ahead.

CHAPTER 6

⁂

School Yourself

YOU'VE RECOGNIZED the talents and gifts fueling your passion. You know that it's your passions that inspire your dreams. You understand that your dreams guide you toward your purpose. Now you're ready for more. You desire to live a life inspired by the pursuit of your dreams. Your new lifestyle, your new business awaits. Now What?

What are the steps you have to take to bring this all together and make your dream journey happen? Just like with any career choice, you start with education – school yourself. If your dream is to become a doctor, you know that you must attend a university, get into medical school, complete residencies and internships, and finally get hired to practice medicine. Your dream may not require you to start school all over again, but find out what you need to know in order be successful and then set out to acquire that knowledge. Assess the intelligence and experience you already have to determine what will be helpful. The primary focus here is to learn and gather information as a foundation for what comes next.

When I decided I was going to leave my corporate life behind and pursue the life of a writer, the first thing I did was research writers and information about the publishing industry. While I had a background in management and marketing, I had no idea what it was like to be a professional writer, nor did I have any understanding of how the book side of the publishing industry worked. I knew that the experience I gained in my years of working with various companies would serve me. I knew business, and I had writing skills, but I didn't know the business of writing, and I knew that if I wanted to be successful, I had some major learning to do. "Being a great cook won't make you a successful restaurant owner." I've said these words countless times. It was time to put what I knew into practice.

For several months I spent countless hours gathering information. I diversified my research and learning processes as much possible. I used the internet, spoke with writers, and connected to people in the publishing industry. I subscribed to publications that were geared to the writers, readers, and the industry as a whole. I learned who the major companies and key players were and started following them. In the mid-2000s, the industry was ripe with literary and publishing events. I attended every local event I could and traveled to those that were out of town. I took writing classes to hone my writing skills and learn techniques from other writers. The more information I gathered, the more I learned, and the more I realized what I still needed to learn.

Once I recognized where I had knowledge gaps, I was able take a more targeted approach to learning. I read books and developed a library of literature that offered additional insight about writing, writers, literature and publishing. I searched for events and seminars. I emailed authors with inquiries and asked some of them to meet and talk with me. I joined writing groups to learn the lingo of the industry and get inside the minds of writers. I worked my way into becoming an insider. I assessed my own experience to determine what would be helpful in my new journey. I knew that my background in marketing would eventually serve me well.

In coupling the information I was learning with the experience I had garnered, an idea struck me. Much of the marketing I'd done in corporate America was working with the events side of the business. I'd spent years working with teams to plan and promote events across multiple industries. I knew that just about every industry had a signature event in which many people from across those industries would come together to share ideas, network, learn from one another, do business and hear from key leaders. There were several events like this in publishing, but none specific enough to help me learn more about operating successfully as a publisher myself.

Opportunities to learn about writing were plentiful, but learning how to publish successfully wasn't easy. My idea was to find a way to bring the publishing industry together so that I could learn best operating practices. So I launched an event for independent publishers. In all my research, I learned there were many others like me who wanted to know more about what it took to be a successful, independent publisher. What better way to learn than to learn directly from those who worked in major publishing houses? Not only could I learn from these industry leaders, I could help other authors and independent publishers learn as well. I may not have known a lot about publishing at the time, but I sure did know a lot about all kinds of corporate events from large scale conferences to intimate workshops. I knew how to plan, market, and sell them. I also knew how important it was to have the right roster of speakers to attract attendees.

I used this experience to create my first successful event

called, The Self-Publishing Symposium. I called in authors, distributors, agents and individuals working in various departments at major publishing houses such as editors, publicists and marketers who were willing to share their expertise. All offered their time at no cost and joined me and 75 other writers interested in establishing successful publishing businesses. I sold sponsorships to companies who were interested in getting in front of writers and independent publishers to help cover the cost of hosting the event. I snagged a media partnership that provided a full-page ad for the event in an issue of their publication. I employed my family to assist with pre-event and day-of responsibilities including registration and the handling of our special guest speakers. I also chose a well-known individual who had built a very successful independent publishing business on her own to serve as our keynote speaker. Every aspiring writer/publisher wanted to hear what she had to say.

This event was extremely successful in helping me learn how to operate a publishing business and allowed me to help other authors acquire the same knowledge. It was the start of many beneficial relationships that I still nurture to this day. I used this event as well as classes, books, groups, conferences and resources to learn as much as I could about my new venture. I was ready for the next step in my journey to turn my dream into a viable business. One of the biggest lessons of all, was that learning never stops.

This part of your journey is like planting seeds. It's where you do more listening than speaking. It's the time to absorb.

Measure Your Progress

In school, taking tests is a way to determine how much you have learned. They are also markers for progress. Although you won't be required to take standardized tests to gauge how much knowledge you've acquired for your dream journey, it's imperative to find ways to confirm that you're applying the knowledge you are receiving in a fruitful way. You'll also need to challenge yourself in order for you to become better, smarter and more savvy.

When I first started writing, I reached out to an author by email to ask for insight. Surprisingly, he emailed me back with some great insight and tips about how I could be successful. He told me that one of the most important things to do is to constantly develop my writing skills. I did some research and found that a pretty successful author was leading a series of writing workshops at a local university. I signed up immediately. At the time, I had only released one book. Family, friends and readers enjoyed the book, and I sold a decent amount of copies. I knew that having my work reviewed and critiqued by professional writers could help me improve my skills.

Attending those writing workshops opened my mind to the possibilities of what I could do with words to make stories more compelling. It also shined a light on my strengths and weaknesses as a writer. I knew I had growing to do as an aspiring author, and after these courses, I knew exactly where I needed to apply my time and energy to get better. I learned interesting techniques for plotting, character development, and ways to pull the reader in that changed the way I wrote for good. That program and every other program I've taken since then, including acquiring a master's in fine arts in Creative Writing, helped me grow as a writer.

Developing your abilities at the most basic level sets the foundation of success early in the process. Don't take short cuts. Gather as much intelligence as you can. I promise you that nothing you could ever learn will be wasted. Most importantly, schooling yourself prepares you for the next phase in the process of turning your dreams into your profession.

As important as it is to learn as much as you can about the path you desire to take, it's equally as important to know when to move on from learning to doing. The learning never stops, but you must know when it's time to grow from one level of learning to the next.

CHAPTER 7

Develop the Dream

NOW THAT YOU have acquired the education, you need to add experience to what you have learned. It's time to begin developing and growing. So what does this actually mean? Your primary focus now is to gain real-world experience and develop and sharpen your skills. Toward the end of this stage the goal is to have earned some credibility and a bit of expertise. Also, the education you already acquired will prepare you for the next stage. This is also the stage where you develop wisdom.

There's a difference between wisdom and knowledge. In the information gathering stage, you've acquired knowledge. Up to this point, much of what you've learned is in theory. Now it is time to apply what you've learned and gain wisdom which comes by doing. The learning process doesn't end. It simply changes. Experiences teach you what books can't.

When I was a starry-eyed aspiring author looking at established authors' lifestyles, I developed visions of grandeur as I gathered information. I assumed so many things about what it was like to live the life of a professional writer based on what I learned. From the outside looking in, the life of an author seemed so glamorous. I dreamed of my books flying off the shelves, traveling around the country on tour signing books at stores with long lines of adoring fans while my titles topped best-seller lists. Then I went from being an aspiring writer to an actual writer and those visions quickly deflated into reality.

Most of my time was spent in isolation behind a computer screen. Sleepless nights gave way to exhausting days from pounding away on my keyboard as I tried to make deadlines. I don't think I signed more than three books at my first signing. I quickly realized I had so much more to learn. I was now living the life of a writer, not imagining what it would be like. Although my initial perception didn't quite match my new real- ity, I was having the time of my life. I was eager to delve deeper and accept every lesson that came my way. I was gaining the hands-on experience I needed to live out my journey to the fullest.

I traveled across the country by plane, train and car. Most of my travel expenses came out of my own pocket even after I was picked up by a major publisher. Yet, every day was a new adven- ture. I continued taking writing classes and applying what I learned to the books I wrote. I could see my writing develop. Over time, I became better at developing characters and creating stronger plots. I fine-tuned the voice of my characters and my ability to tell a compelling story got better after every book. I saw the difference and could feel it as I wrote. My readers noticed as well. Some were sure to let me know.

Eventually, aspiring writers sought me out to gain my insight. Media outlets became interested in not just my books, but the story about my journey to becoming a writer. When I was invited to attend a literary festival in the Caribbean with all expenses paid, I knew I'd made significant process. They flew me in, covered the cost of my hotel at a beautiful seaside resort, and asked that I facilitate a workshop and sit on a panel to talk about the writing process.

I still spent many hours in front of my computer in isolation. I sold more books at signings, some of which were well attended, others were not. The important thing was that I gained experience and developed wisdom about what the life of a writer truly entailed.

In addition to writing, I offered consulting services to entrepreneurs and small businesses, helping them develop branding and marketing campaigns. After working as a marketing professional for large and midsized companies, I was able to help smaller companies build their brands and promote their products and services. My first contract was a barter agreement. I offered my expertise in exchange for the opportunity to learn more about the publishing industry from the inside. Contracting with that small publisher to develop an integrated marketing campaign was a win-win. They got the help they needed and I gained experience. The opportunity also taught me other vital skills like contract negotiation and how to best manage client relationships. By the time I took on my next client, I'd upgraded my contract, tweaked my services, and was able to charge more profitable rates because I now had quality references.

I continued to hone my skills, nurturing my gift of writing. I developed a working knowledge of the industry and how to become successful. I'd begun the process of developing expertise. I gained valuable experience and credibility. The more I engaged, the more I worked my way toward becoming an authority in the areas of my skillset. Most importantly, I was walking in my dream. There was still so much to do.

I started to make money from the writing. My growth and experiences fueled my confidence in the fact that I could build a viable business based on my gifts, passions and dreams.

I learned valuable lessons in this phase that set the stage for the possibility of increasing earned income. Obtaining feedback was vital. Though it was challenging to hear critiques of my writing, it helped me improve my writing skills. While working with clients on consulting agreements, feedback helped me tweak the guidance I provided so they could experience better outcomes. Other times, feedback offered me a different perspective that I may not have originally considered. Speaking of perspective, I found that obtaining feedback from different vantage points was greatly beneficial. When it came to writing, I wanted to hear from readers, editors, media and other writers. As a consultant, running my ideas by mentors or other consultants was helpful in numerous ways from improving my services to making critical changes to my contracts. Hearing directly from my clients helped to ensure that our relationship and agreements remained mutually beneficial.

Most importantly, it helped me understand if what I offered was worth the value I assigned to it. With the feedback I was given, I made adjustments that increased my ability to deliver better results.

I was able to develop credibility with my current audience and proved to new audiences that I was worthy to engage with. As my credibility grew, so did my confidence and comfort level. This was important, as now I was able to begin putting my unique stamp on the work I did. I garnered a reputation for quality, and for delivering effectiveness and efficiency.

By the later part of this stage, I had further developed a style and my voice as a writer. I was able to sufficiently communicate how the services I offered through consulting were distinct. I had achieved measurable results, a proven track record, and testimonials that spoke to my proficiencies. As a writing instructor and facilitator, I discovered how to best help my students understand and apply the concepts I taught them. My ability to create engaging lessons and impactful curriculum had improved considerably. I established great relationships and my interpersonal skills were sharper than ever before. I assessed my strengths and weakness and worked toward continuous improvement.

I loved what I was doing, but my income was inconsistent. I needed to make a better living. I didn't want to go back to corporate America so I had to find a way to make this dream profitable and sustainable. It was time to raise the stakes because I wanted to continue to get paid for doing what I loved now that I knew it was possible.

The ultimate reward was showing my children what it looked like to live my dream. Just like any parent wanting the best for their kids, I constantly told them that they could do anything they wanted if they just worked hard. I encouraged them to follow their hearts and pursue their dreams. Showing them was so much more impactful that telling them. I couldn't be a hypocrite and tell them to chase their dreams while I deferred my own. It was important that they saw me work hard, grow, fail, overcome, achieve and persevere. They witnessed firsthand all the joys and sacrifices it took for me to make my dreams come true.

Life had changed considerably for me. My days were more productive and meaningful. My levels of stress decreased significantly. The flexibility in my schedule and the sense of autonomy was freeing. The passion I had for the work I was doing was evident to anyone whose path I crossed. The ability to choose who I wanted to work with was incredible. Every win and new opportunity reinforced the fact that I was doing the right things. I didn't want to live any other way.

I was ready for the next step. I knew it would require new levels of learning and growing as well as sacrifice. I was up for the challenge.

CHAPTER 8

❧

*P*ackage Your Passion

YOU'VE IDENTIFIED your passions and dreams. You've gathered information to learn more about the business you're getting into. You gained vital experience, earned creditability and developed a bit of expertise. You've also gotten a taste of what it's like to earn money doing what you love. Now, you're ready to level up and make your dream profitable and sustainable. It's time to talk about packaging your passion and preparing to build your business.

The leap between the last stage and this one is quite large. It's very possible to develop your dream and make some extra income from it. However taking it from something that you do on the side to building a business that is profitable and sustainable is quite different. This state requires a deeper level of discipline, commitment, resources, investment and sacrifice. Yet, the outcome, the rewards and return on investment are also greater. As you move into an increased level of commitment, it's imperative to ensure that what you build from here is in alignment with your talents, passions, dream and purpose.

Making a living dictates your lifestyle. Before you actually get to the point where you can make a living and change your lifestyle, you'll have to get strategic and learn best practices for building your business.

Packaging your passion is what you need to do to make your business profitable. It's an imperative stage where you begin to strategically develop your products, services and offerings. Gather all that you've learned and all that you've experienced. Make the appropriate adjustments based on your feedback and trials. You'll need all of it to create a valuable and sellable product or service or develop a profitable way to share your intellectual property. Here's where you'll generate something from your passion that can be utilized to develop your business further.

Ask yourself what you can create that is distinct and provides value to your customer or end user. How can it become profitable enough for you to build a business? What you produce on this level is not the same as what you may have developed previously. It has to be bigger, better, and scalable. Scalability is essential. How will you handle increased interest or demand? How do you make this work for you? Seriously consider the following questions:

- What do you have to offer a customer base?
- Is it a product?
- Do you have a service to offer?
- Do you have some kind of intellectual property that will help your client or customer increase a skillset or develop personally or professionally?
- Why would people be interested in what you're selling?

- What makes it different than other products and services?
- What will the product, service or intellectual property look like?
- What unique spin can you place on what you're providing?
- What is your unique story?
- How does your story relate to the product?
- What is the message you have for your clients, customers or end users?
- What is the impact your offer will have on your users?
- How can you best package it?
- How will you communicate the benefit of your offer?
- How will you make your offer scalable?
- What systems will you use to develop, deliver and manage your offer?
- Do you have the resources to move forward?
- How can you obtain the resources needed to build your business?

At this stage you'll need to do another level of research. Find individuals or business that offer similar products or services and study them. Study their process, distribution, delivery, marketing and branding as much as you can. This is about learning best practices from entities that are succeeding in areas where you want to succeed. This is not about taking what they're producing and reproducing it. Your offering is distinct because your stamp is on it. This is about learning to succeed in business.

Time is essential here as well. Lack of time is one of the most utilized excuses as to why people don't pursue their dreams. The reality is that we make time for those things we prioritize in our lives. Set aside the necessary time to make this happen. Dedicate a few hours a week to working towards your goal. I always say that if you carry a brick a day, one day you'll have enough bricks to build a house. Our dream journeys are the same way. Consistency is key. Discipline is vital. One brick every day and one day you'll be able to build a house. Your effort and frequency will dictate your outcome. When you put in the work, all you have to do is trust the process and things will manifest.

Systems and tools are also essential in this part of the process. These days, there are numerous programs and apps to help get business done more efficiently. For instance, I am not a numbers person and have always begrudged the time I had to spend managing my books on my own. I'd spend hours trying to get things right until I finally starting using accounting programs. These systems automated the process for me and cut the amount of time I spent trying to reconcile budgets and expenses by at least seventy-five percent. As a writer, I spent countless hours editing my content. I've employed editing tools to help improve my texts and eliminate certain steps from the editing process. I still spend a lot of time editing because it's essential for a writer, however the tools help make the process more efficient with the end result of fewer errors. Determine what systems can help you become more efficient with your business and time.

Consider the story of Nyakio Kamoche Grieco, founder of the Nyakio Beauty skin care line. Although Nyakio worked in the entertainment industry, she had a passion for research and discovery. Born in America with Kenyan roots, Nyakio grew up spending summers with her grandmother, a coffee farmer in Kenya. She learned skin care and beauty regimens watching her grandmother crush coffee beans and use oils and sugar cane to cleanse and exfoliate her skin.

Years later, Nyakio graduated with a degree in business and pursued a career in entertainment but was called back to her roots with a desire to develop her own skin care line. Using what her grandmother taught her, she began creating products right in her kitchen. Initially, she shared her creations with family and friends. She eventually launched her line of skin care products. She caught the attention of Ellen DeGeneres and Oprah Winfrey and the unexpected happened. Nyakio had to shut her business down. She couldn't handle the increased demand for her beauty products after exposure by the two powerhouses generated so much interest.

There's a stark difference in making products in your kitchen and selling them to fill orders for wide distribution to the masses. Nyakio regrouped and reworked her business, eventually securing investor relationships and distribution deals with large scale retail outlets. Her beauty line is now manufactured and distributed by Unilever and her line can be found in major retail stores across America such as Target and Ulta.

For Nyakio to go from mixing bottles of product in her kitchen to mass distribution in several countries across the globe it took a completely different level of commitment, discipline and resources. She scaled up with her business. Everyone's vision is not to become an international brand. Your goal may be to take your dream from a side hustle to something you do full time. You may desire to become an entrepreneur or establish a large business. Regardless of what you envision, it's important to take your passions and dreams and create something sellable and scalable so that you can make a living and change your lifestyle.

Impact is equally important. Remember, when you're building a business that's tied to your purpose, you must consider impact as much as profitability. How will what you create align with your purpose? What value can it bring to someone else's life? How will it bring meaning or fulfilment to you? Without considering these questions, you're just pursuing another job.

Nyakio wanted to do more than just make money. She made

a decent enough salary in entertainment. Surely with hard work she would continue to earn more money and gain experience in her industry. However, what Nyakio has is so much deeper. She's helping women look and feel beautiful using green and clean products. I can personally attest to the fact that she's using her time and resources to be a beacon of light and service to girls across America with the support she provides to nonprofit organizations like Girls, Inc. She's also able to enjoy a profound connection with her grandmother in her daily work. Who wouldn't want to get paid for that?

My passion was to write and teach writing. My dream was to become an author and entertain, inform and provide a great escape from the woes of this world. My purpose is to inspire others to live out their dreams like I'm doing with mine. My purpose opened the doors to new ways to impact lives and I started working with people both young and older. I educated myself and acquired experience. I developed my dream by activating what I learned and deepening my experience. As a result, I wrote books and consulted individuals on developing brands and marketing plans. However, when it was time to scale up to create something more than a side hustle, I had to consider the how, the why and the impact.

As an individual, I would only do what I could physically get done on my own. Scaling up meant growing while keeping a balance between profitability and impact. I got serious about my talent, growth, and the opportunities that could stem from them. Instead of writing a book every now and then, I created a plan and dedicated more time to producing books to meet a growing demand from readers. I developed campaigns designed to increase visibility for my books and brand as an author. I created measurable goals, assessed them and made adjustments to ensure that my goals were met. I incorporated activities and events that would allow me to meet new and larger audiences of readers. I connected with other authors, industry professionals and brands to maximize my exposure to readers and I constantly invested in my brand to increase visibility across all platforms.

It worked for me. I went from reaching out to bookstores, event producers and media outlets to being contacted by them to get involved with what they had going on. Part of my strategic development plan to increase my audience included writing in new genres. Until this point, I had published some books independently and others were picked up by small publishers. By the time I had the opportunity to pitch a series of books to an editor at one of the largest publishers of romance fiction, she had begun asking other writers about my interest in writing romance. Harlequin initially offered me a two-book deal followed by a six-book deal and another two-book deal on a new imprint. We're currently in negotiations for my newest deal. My advance and royalties increased with each contract.

When it came to teaching, I went from facilitating a few workshops here and there to developing writing and literacy curriculum and leading writing residencies for the New York City Department of Education. After a return to graduate school to acquire a Master of Fine Arts in Creative Writing, I began teaching at the university level as an adjunct and visiting professor.

As a marketing and brand consultant, I went from exchanging hours for services with a small magazine publisher to managing multiple clients. My background in successfully building my own brand plus more than a decade of experience as a marketing professional was beneficial. However, the unique spin I offered based on my journey is what really attracted clients—big company strategies on a small company budget.

Finally, in fulfilling my passion of serving youth, I ultimately became the executive director of a nonprofit organization with a mission to serve and advocate on behalf of girls.

I packaged my passion by developing writing curriculum

that not only taught literacy techniques but was also empowering and challenged social injustices through words, combining my passion for writing and working with youth. If my schedule didn't allow me to teach my own lessons, I hired facilitators who were capable of delivering the material with an equal passion for teaching and empowering youth.

I had packaged my passion with know-how, skills, a unique story and purpose. I delivered on what I promised and offered value to those I worked with. I served happy, satisfied clients and taught children to love reading and writing. I'd made a name for myself and set expectations that I often exceeded. I worked toward excellence and sought out opportunities until eventually people sought me out for opportunities. I spent my days writing, teaching and working with youth. This was a long way from working through rough days on jobs that I hated or walking through life without purpose. I was doing what I loved and getting paid, but I also knew there was more.

Planning is key, but in addition to planning for success, it's important to be strategic. Don't just put together a checklist of things you think you should do to reach your goal. Strategize. Delve deeper here. Outline what you will do. Figure out how you will do it. Determine why you're doing it and then measure, track and evaluate your progress on your way to success. That's the only way to truly move forward, by making informed decisions and planning to measure, track and evaluate your progress.

CHAPTER 9

❧

𝓕rom Passion to Profits

THE BRIDGE between passion and profits is a platform. In packaging my passion and sharing it with the world I ended up establishing a platform. That platform opened the door to additional revenue streams.

What exactly is a platform? Your platform is your declaration that you make to the world about the principles on which you stand. It becomes part of the basis of what you become known for.

For example, as a writer I spend a lot of time working with people of all ages, especially youth. My goal was to teach them literacy skills and evoke a love of reading and writing. More importantly, I wanted to inspire them. I wanted them to use reading and literacy as a tool for expression, advocacy and empowerment because that's what I was passionate about. My background as a professional award-winning writer lent credibility to what I represented. This led to speaking opportunities where I encouraged youth. Almost by default, I encouraged the adults around those youth and eventually began doing speaking engagements for adults at schools, conferences and events. The more I taught and spoke, the more I became known for empowering people in general and women more specifically. I'd become associated with principles around literacy, motivation, and empowerment, resulting in the creation of my platform.

Once my platform was established, individuals, media and businesses called on me to work with them based on these principles and what people believed I delivered. Each opportunity reinforced these principles and strengthened my platform, authenticating me as an authority in the areas of writing and empowerment. Soon, people wanted to know more about how I did what I'd done rather than what I did or what I taught. As I began to share my experiences, this added personal and professional development to my platform making it a fertile basis for how I showed up in the world. It encapsulates the fullness of what I've become known for, while reinforcing my credibility, skills and brand overall.

Platforms can be created by default or design. A well-developed platform becomes your brand and can produce opportunities, many of which can be revenue generating. As I mentioned, mine started by default and then I approached it more strategically and developed it by design. Now, when institutions and individuals are looking for someone to deliver a powerful message of empowerment or lend a voice to conversations around empowerment, I get called. When schools want help getting students to learn literacy techniques, foster a love of reading and empower their students at the same time, I get called. When companies want to align their brands with another brand that is authoritative when it comes to empowerment, social justice, and personal and professional development, I get called. When individuals, entrepreneurs and business leaders want to better understand how to build businesses and lead with passion, I get called.

It all started with my passion for writing and inspiring others and developed into so much more. Now I'm able to earn money through multiple revenue streams based on my platform. Those streams come from writing, teaching, speaking and coaching. My platform also affords me other indirect sources of income now as an influencer. Simply stated, an influencer is someone an audience listens to, and they value what that person has to say. As an influencer, one can convince or persuade their audience to engage in certain behaviors, participate in experiences, and purchase products or services that align with their platform or brand. This opens doors to perks, opportunities and yes, more revenue streams.

Monetizing Your Passion

This is often the hard part. It's much easier for people to build a viable platform, but getting paid for what they bring to the table gets tricky based on what they are offering. I know this through my experience as a coach and by interviewing a plethora of women who have turned their dreams into their businesses. For many, this was one of the most challenging aspects.

The easy part is the research. Find out the range of what other people are charging for similar products or services and determine where you'd like to stand. For starters, considering your level of experience, the amount of time you put into production, and other normal business factors will help you come up with reasonable pricing. If you're producing tangible products, it's easier to calculate the cost of doing business. However, when you're offering services established through your intellectual property, it often becomes a lot harder.

When I started my career as an author, I published my first

three books independently. It didn't take much for me to determine the price point for my books because that industry has an established formula. Novels are priced based on the number of words and whether or not they were hardcover, paperback and eventually digital. Every version has a price range. Other factors that determined pricing are genre or materials used to produce the book.

The hard part was trying to figure out the right price to charge for more intangible products such as speaking and coaching services. I'd often factor in what I thought I was worth and many times I missed the mark because I was afraid to charge too much. Like so many others whom I worked with in the journey, we felt we were doing what we loved. We were indulging our dreams. We were passionate. Many of us did these same things for free and now we had to determine a value to assign to it? This felt awkward. Collectively, we realized that our passion for the work wasn't the problem. It was what we believed we were worth that was the issue. It was the fact that we couldn't properly perceive our value. As a result, we were giving the business away. Some practically worked for free.

You can't build a business if you don't make money. I recall one coaching client who was building her nonprofit business. She was truly passionate about the mission and committed to the vision. She was adamant about helping the people she served to the best of her ability. She just wasn't making any money. When we examined all that was happening, I realized she wasn't charging nearly enough to carry out her services. Not only was she not getting paid for any of the time she put into managing the business, she wasn't properly calculating the cost of resources needed for each program she delivered. Instead of making money, she lost on every project and those monies often had to come out of her pocket.

When I challenged her to raise the cost of her programs, she felt bad about charging more despite putting in countless hours to coordinate her programs. I explained that her feelings wasn't going to keep her in business very long. It was her inability to see the value of what she was bringing to the table that was the problem. Fixing her value problem fixed her money problem.

In interviewing the various women mentioned throughout this book about setting their value, I found that many of them found this hard to do. Each of them loved what they did. Each of them wanted to get paid for doing what they loved. All of them built great businesses. And all of them struggled through this part of the process. I recall when coach and motivational speaker Abiola Abrams transitioned from a television personality to author and ultimately to fulfilling her dream of becoming a spirit-led coach. Conversations around the struggle of figuring out the right price point dominated several of our meetings. Now Abiola leads world-wide retreats. She coaches entrepreneurs and provides programs to help change mindsets and build businesses. She's not shy about the value she brings or her ability to change lives. And her clients aren't shy about paying her what she's worth.

When people know their value, they can charge and get what they ask for. Here's an easy comparison. As consumers, we place value on things all the time. Let's take shoes for example. We're willing to pay higher prices for a pair of shoes we perceive to have a certain value or are made by a certain designer. The shoes can be similar in materials and style. However, we are willing to pay a much higher price for specific brands based on a value we've bought into. That designer has stated that they are worth a certain price point. They considered the cost of business and materials, and created a perception that their product is worth what they're asking. And those of us who are interested in their products agree with the perception they established when we purchase their product because they believed it was worth it. People are always willing to pay more when they believe they're getting more.

Here are some of the things we consider when we factor in value; level and amount of experience, background, credentials, status, popularity and access. We will pay more to a person with ten years of experience than we will to a person with three years of experience. Credentials such as certifications or degrees are often indicators of higher priced services. We have witnessed prices rise due to the popularity of a product or service. And, we have perceived things that are exclusive to be of a higher value and will pay for access to things that other people may not have access to.

Consider how what you're offering will help your customers. Will it help them save time? Will it provide a certain level of convenience? Will what you're offering help soothe pain points in their lives? Will it increase their knowledge base? People will pay for products and services that save them time, offer convenience, or help them manage some difficult aspect of their lives or business. Use the feedback you acquired in the 'Developing the Dream' stage to help answer some of these questions.

As the value of what you offer increases, so do your prices. To ensure that you get repeat business, it's best that you "over deliver." I don't mean charge less that what you're providing. I mean, give your customers more than they expect with great service and a few amazing perks. They will feel like they have received more than what they paid for and look forward to doing business with you again.

Do your research. Understand the value you bring. Know your cost of doing business, including time, materials and resources. Set your price making sure that it's reasonable and fair, and that it reflects the value you've assigned to it. Be confident in the price you've set and stick with it! As your value increases, make sure your prices increase along with it. You may have to make some adjustments until your products develop a base. Remember that whatever value you set for your product or service you need to back that up with delivering on what you've promised with excellence. Be careful to keep your pricing within the range of similar products or services. Don't overprice and don't sell yourself short.

Why is monetizing your passion appropriately important? Our income is a major indicator of the kind of lifestyle we live. It's not simply about making a lot of money, but if you want to develop a profession or business from your passions and dreams, you need to understand how to scale up your passion beyond a good side hustle. For the business to be successful, it needs to be sustainable. Good business practices are necessary to keep the business viable, hence, keeping the dream alive. It's impossible to stay in business if your business isn't profitable.

CHAPTER 10

❧

*G*et the Word Out

SEVERAL YEARS AGO, Dr. Michele C. Reed hired me to help her build her brand. She'd already fulfilled her childhood dream of becoming a doctor, yet her work inspired other dreams. Dr. Reed, now endearingly known as Fit Doc, found that she was also passionate about helping her patients lead better lives physically, mentally and spiritually.

When we started working together, Dr. Reed had received invitations to provide commentary to the media, write for medical websites and publications, and speak at wellness events. Yet she hadn't developed her brand. In fact, she didn't have much beyond business cards.

Over the next several months, I worked with Dr. Reed to develop her brand. We identified what her platform would represent and developed a strategic branding campaign that included a new website and social media marketing. Maximizing every component of that branding campaign, Dr. Reed quickly established her brand as an authority in women's health and fitness. People now had several places to go to find out more about her. Her brand now includes fitness classes and a product line of materials. She's appeared on numerous television shows, local and national news broadcasts, and in multiple print publications. She hosts annual fitness retreats and has established a sizable following across her social media platforms. All from being consistent about getting the word out about who she was and what she did.

My marketing and branding career started back in the late nineties. And though many of the methods we use to market have changed, the foundation of marketing and branding hasn't. Understanding these two concepts can seem a bit confusing to those who don't have a background in marketing and branding. Marketing comprises the actions a business takes to promote products or services to a targeted audience. Experienced marketers use the 'marketing mix' better known as the Four Ps of marketing, product, price, place and promotions to develop effective marketing plans. Branding is a practice of marketing that identifies people, goods and services, and differentiates them from competitors. It is a key component of product management in the marketing mix. Companies invest a lot of thought and resources into developing and distinguishing their brands.

Other marketing practices include advertising, collateral development, promotional efforts, public relations, event marketing and more. However, for the purpose of this text, we will focus on branding. As part of the Packaging Your Passion chapter, we discussed developing a platform which comprised a set of principles by which one becomes known for. We also talked about distinguishing yourself from others in your field. That is what branding is all about. And once you know what your brand is and what it promises, you can be strategic and effective about building and promoting that brand.

Branding is a huge concept which includes everything from product development to logo design to strategic management. For the purposes of this book, I'll focus on the aspects that are more likely to meet your needs as a person building a profession or business based on your passions and dreams. To establish a strong brand you'll have to get really clear on the purpose of your business. Then I'd recommend the following steps.

1. Determine how you want your brand to be perceived.
2. Establish your unique message or 'brand story.'
3. Communicate & promote your message
4. Be consistent.

Dr. Reed determined that she wanted to be perceived as more than a medical professional. She had a passion for helping patients achieve total health both inside and outside of her office. She was also passionate about helping patients avoid or better manage chronic health conditions. Her goal was to help her patients medically and help them lead fit and healthy lifestyles. She didn't just talk about it to her patients; she created opportunities for them to join her in various activities to achieve fit lifestyles.

Dr. Reed isn't the average doctor, and her brand exemplifies that. She didn't become a doctor because the medical profession paid well. She was motivated by a desire to impact her community. This was part of her brand story and communicating this helped to steer how her brand was perceived.

Dr. Reed communicated and promoted her messaging with an integrated approach, which is the most effective way to market. Relying on one method of marketing will prevent you from fully reaching your target audience and diminish your ability to get your message across to as many people as possible.

To get the word out and build her brand, Dr. Reed created a website, and engaged in social media marketing, live events, speaking engagements, podcasts, and so much more. Each practice afforded her the opportunity to reinforce her message with her current audience while reaching new audiences.

Lastly, Dr. Reed was consistent in communicating her message in a relevant way through all efforts until her brand was well established, and she continues to do so today. Consistency is essential in communicating your message and establishing a brand. You can find Dr. Reed sharing important medical information in books, on television, at events, across social media platforms and in print publications. Every encounter creates an opportunity for her to reinforce who she is perceived to be. Her message and presence is consistent, resulting in a healthy following and a strong brand.

Although the principles of marketing remain unchanged, the methods used tend to change frequently. Stay abreast of the latest tools that you can use to market effectively. I remember when print ads were popular, though costly. Then getting banner ads became the thing to do. Depending on what you offer, live events are still very important. Establishing an authoritative voice helps strengthen your brand. Offer commentary on subjects where you've developed expertise. This helps establish your credibility and grow your audience. Having a strong social media presence is effective and can be lucrative. Developing a community that you engage with is imperative to your success. People are looking for engagement. Diversifying your methods of reaching your audience will ensure that you've connected with them in the ways they prefer.

The days of the hard sell are over. If you sell dog food, don't get on social media and talk about how much your dog food costs. Instead, talk about how dogs enrich your life. Be that doting doggy parent on your profiles. Post pictures of you playing fetch with your pet or taking them for walks. Offer tips on how to keep your dog happy and healthy. Then, you can speak about how much your dog likes the food you sell and you'll generate sales. But most importantly, be authentic. You must first establish a rapport with your community. Once you build trust with your audience, they are more likely to engage with you in various ways. It's like building relationships.

I would also encourage you to use systems and tools to help you market your brand as consistently and efficiently as possible. Have an email list so you can reach your audience. Utilize text messaging platforms that work for your audience. There are a host of marketing and social media tools to help you manage this aspect of your business. Programs like Hootsuite and Planoly can help you manage your social media profiles. Other programs will help with creating videos and graphics or provide templates for marketing. Get help when you need it.

Understand that your messaging will reach three types of audiences. The first is your community of customers or clients. These are your end users. These are the people who use or benefit directly from your product or service. The next audience category is the gatekeepers. Gatekeepers can open the 'gate' and provide you with access to large numbers of clients, customers or members of your community. Using our furry little friends as an example, you can reach dog lovers directly, or you can reach gatekeepers such as pet shop owners, bloggers, or vets. This will help amplify your message and allow you to reach more people than you may currently have access to. The last audience category is the media. Don't leave the media out of your strategic plans just because they're harder to gain access to. They are also gatekeepers, but they are a different kind of community to engage. Communicating your message through the media will enhance your brand exposure while adding credibility to your platform. These strategies will help you become a brand that people want to trust in and want to engage in.

Strategize on the best ways to reach all three audiences with your messaging using an integrated approach to best saturate your marketing base. You don't want to leave anyone out because that leaves money on the table.

Use every method of marketing and branding possible, email, mailings, social media, events, and advertising. Determine your budget and decide the most cost effective options. Your audience will have diverse preferences for how they like to receive information and you don't want your customers to miss your message. Social media is extremely popular and very effective. Yet, people on social media are constantly inundated with information. It's important to be strategic. Frequency matters. Share your message often through these various formats, but pace yourself so you don't generate fatigue amongst your customer base. You want customers to see your materials and you want to engage them, but you don't want them to unsubscribe or unfriend you because you're bugging them. There's a delicate balance between informing, reminding, and inundating your consumer. Create professional or business profiles for your business or brand and engage with your audience in a way that informs and offers value. Depending on your brand, this will not be the place to share funny or borderline inappropriate memes.

CHAPTER 11

$\mathcal{S}$ ustainability & Service

NOW THAT YOUR business is up and running, you have to keep it running. It's bigger than you now. Focus on strategy, sustainability, and pacing your growth. Your goal is to continuously deliver excellent service. Pay attention to your customer's and client's needs so you can fulfill them and respond to changes when necessary. Upgrade and refresh your products and services. Give your customers a reason to come back. Serve your audience. Develop your expertise.

Your core values should be your purpose. Serve your customer base in the best way possible, on a consistent basis, and the money will come. Don't be shy about getting paid, but never forget that the reason for being in business is greater than getting a check. Your divine assignment is to use your gifts.

We touched on strategy when it comes to planning. However, being strategic in business overall is vital to keeping your business going. Keep a strategic mindset about your company's growth, the use of your resources and your ability to serve your audience base. Learn your industry. Watch the trends navigating through your industry. Be aware of the tools that will help you run your business more efficiently.

This is an area where many entrepreneurs fall short, especially those who are not leading staff. Yes, you're operating in your gift. Yes, you're enjoying the fact that you're getting paid for doing what you love. However, you need to take your business seriously in order for it to be successful and sustainable. You don't have to be the next Amazon unless you want to. When Jeff Bezos started selling books in his garage, the Amazon we know today was not part of his initial vision. Your focus should be on your purpose and serving your customer. Jeff wanted to get books into people's hands, but planning, strategy, commitment, and good business practices prepared him to take advantage of opportunities that he had never imagined.

The same goes for Madam C. J. Walker. She wanted to help women grow their hair. Estee Lauder wanted to help women look, smell and feel good about themselves. Both woman sold their products door to door and built empires. You may not desire an empire. Your vision of what success looks like may be very different. The most important thing to know is that however you define success, you can achieve it.

SHOW UP FOR YOU!

I had always been a great employee. I took initiative, took assignments seriously and strived for excellence. What I delivered often exceeded expectations and goals. I put in numerous hours every single week, and often worked late even when I wasn't getting paid for it. I'm a team player. As a visionary I always saw the possibilities in every opportunity. As a creative person, I enjoyed coming up with new ideas and campaigns. There were many times when I outperformed my peers or impressed my boss with my dedication and vigor. When necessary, I rolled up my sleeves and jumped in the trenches to get the job done.

I worked hard to develop my leadership style based on what I perceived were some of the best attributes from the leaders I reported to. Setting a collaborative and cohesive tone was important to me. I wanted my employees to want to come to work. I helped them reach their best potential. Part of my goal as a manager was to help my staff members grow and develop. It was exciting for me to see them master personal and professional goals. My employees knew that their voices mattered, and they felt valued. I gave the companies I worked for my all, even on the jobs I hated. I showed up for the staff and I showed up for the team. I did my part and often went the extra mile.

I was dedicated and that dedication led to great results. Things didn't always go well. I made mistakes, but learned from them. I failed at times, but got back up, got back in the game and pressed on. While I received a paycheck for the time I put in, my company reaped the rewards of my hard work and consistent dedication.

When I started working for myself I didn't mind putting in the work, but I wasn't always consistent. I set aside time to complete tasks, but wasn't disciplined in the same way I had been when I was employed by someone else's company. I'd set goals and work toward achieving, but didn't always apply the same fervor as when I worked for other companies. As a result, my outcomes weren't consistent because my efforts weren't consistent.

When I really applied myself, my business did well. When I wasn't as committed to meeting my goals, progress slowed considerably. I realized the problem. I wasn't taking business seriously, because I wasn't taking myself seriously. I showed up for corporations, but I wasn't showing up for me or for my dream. I wasn't putting the same energy into working, planning, strategizing, and committing myself to results. I did these same things every single day working for others. But my consistency was less than lackluster when it came to myself.

Competency wasn't my issue. I was definitely capable. I had proven my skills and knowledge time and time again in other positions. If I wanted to enjoy consistent success, I had to commit to putting in the work. Quitting had never been an option before, so I couldn't quit on myself.

Successful businesses don't come by way of sheer luck. They are developed. This is especially important for individuals who want to build viable businesses from their dreams. The journey is often so personal for us that we have to remind ourselves to run ours as a business.

Planning, strategy, consistency and discipline is where successful businesses begin and thrive. Professional development is how good business leaders become great leaders. Build a library of information detailing the successes of other businesses. Connect with other business leaders. Learn from mentors and engage those coming up behind you. Stay abreast of what's happening in your industry. Pay attention to how outside factors impact your business. This is how we continue to cultivate a business mindset. If we can get up every day to show up for work in someone else's company, then we can show up every day for our own.

Think strategically about every area of business to ensure that you're making the decisions that will offer you the best possible outcomes. This way you will make efficient use of your time and resources and yield greater results. In business, everything is strategic.

Karma is Currency

Here's the part where we get a bit more spiritual. Another successful business strategy is giving back. This may sound a bit esoteric, but it's effective. Creating good karma around your business is not just a good thing to do, but it will directly impact your bottom line. This is why many corporations have a department dedicated to social responsibility.

There's multiple ways you can give back. And if you make this part of your business practice, you'll see opportunities to reap huge benefits. Here's an example. As a book-lover, writer, and empowerment advocate, I decided to give back to my community by offering a college scholarship to high school students. It's a small amount, but when we're talking about the cost of education in America, we know that every penny counts. At a certain time every year I release information about the scholarship and invite students to apply. I also focus on celebrating the students who win the scholarship. Each time, I've seen an increase in book sales. It's just like people who like to support companies who are environmentally responsible. Even the finance industry uses this strategy to sell investments. Investors can chose to put their money into options that are 'green' or have proven to be socially or environmentally responsible.

Generally, customers feel good about purchasing your products or services when they know you support charitable efforts or communities. Customers feel like they're putting their money to good use. Businesses benefit from positive PR and you'll feel great about your ability to impact your community or favorite charity. As a business leader in the nonprofit community, I've witnessed first-hand how consumers deliberately target companies who give back to their communities and have made some of these companies their business of choice for their products or services.

Also, help others on their journey to success. When we help others, we actually widen the doors of opportunity for ourselves. Giving of our time, resources and wisdom is in direct alignment with fulfilling our purpose. It's our responsibility as business citizens.

Various scriptures throughout the Bible speak to being generous and the impact of that generosity. *"Remember this: Whoever sows sparingly will also reap sparingly, and whoever sows generously will also reap generously. Each of you should give what you have decided in your heart to give, not reluctantly or under compulsion, for God loves a cheerful giver. And God is able to bless you abundantly so that in all things and all times, having all that you need, you will abound in every good work." 2 Corinthians 9: 6-8 NIV.*

"A generous person will prosper; whoever refreshes others will be refreshed." Proverbs 11:25 NIV.

"Give and it will be given to you. A good measure, pressed down, shaken together, and running over will be poured into your lap. For with the measure you use, it will be measured back to you." Luke 6:39 NIV.

I could go on with biblical references of generosity, but I'll stop there. So giving back is not just good business practice, it's spiritually sound. Take a look at most major corporations across all industries such as technology, finance and retail. They all have divisions in their corporations dedicated to community and/or social responsibility, and a number of them have established foundations. They serve the community, and the community serves them right back.

As a business leader, I constantly read books that offer advice, inspiration and tips. Out of many, the most profound business book I've ever read was *The Go Giver* by Bob Burg and John David Mann. A salesman wanted to learn how to be more successful in sales and was moved to reach out to one of the greatest businessman in his community. This businessman agreed to mentor the sales executive who expected to learn his secret for highly effective sales strategies. Instead, to his surprise, the businessman taught him much more about how to be a giver than a salesman. The key to the businessman's renowned success was his generosity. Using the principles he was taught, the salesman ultimately became a great success.

It's possible that you never anticipated that giving would be one of the principles discussed in this book when, in fact, giving has been a major factor in the success of so many people and businesses. If you haven't already done so, I urge you to make generosity a key part of your business strategy. You won't be disappointed. The potential returns are too numerous to name. The important thing to take away here is to know that giving back directly impacts your business in a positive way. Make allowances for giving back using your time or resources. Your business will be better for it.

CHAPTER 12

$\mathcal{T}$he Lifestyle

CONGRATULATIONS! You're ready to live your very own Dream Journey, a lifestyle inspired by the pursuit of your dreams. How exciting! We've covered everything from realizing your talents, indulging your passions, chasing your dreams, fulfilling your purpose, and building your business. We outlined how it's all connected. Then we explored the actual steps you need to take to build your profession or your business based on your dreams. Before we wrap this up, I want to touch on a few other tidbits and experiences that you'll have to navigate as you live out your Dream Journey.

I'll start with a few hard truths. This journey is not easy. It's filled with ups and downs and will take lots of hard work, dedication, and commitment. But again, if you have been working hard to make someone's business successful, you can certainly work hard to make your own business successful. You will experience hardship and setbacks. Understand that there are no losses in this journey, only learnings. You will try things and fail. Remember that failure is an effective teacher. It shows you what doesn't work and brings you steps closer to what does work. Companies pivot to new strategies all the time.

There were plenty of days when I wanted to throw in the towel. And from where I stand today, I'm so glad I didn't. Never quit your dream. No empire was built in a day. Have patience with yourself and your progress. If you are consistent and disciplined, you will see results. Trust the process.

It's okay not to have all the answers. That's why there's a library full of business books. Talk to people. Find your tribe. Get a mentor that can offer insight periodically. When you find that you have knowledge or skill gaps, seek out qualified, reliable people that can help you fill them.

Building a great business feels great. Never let your ego get in the way of your progress. Always be willing to listen or learn. You never know where your next great idea can come from. Don't compare your journey to the next person because your story is way too unique. It's better to try and fail, than to never try at all and rob yourself of experiencing all the amazing possibilities of growing.

Be sure to celebrate your wins. You worked for them and deserve to recognize how far you've come. Celebrating gives you time to stop what you're doing and live in the moment. Life can get so hectic sometimes that we feel like we can't stop. If we do, something will fall apart. It won't. Allowing yourself to live in the moment lets you truly feel the joy of winning. Don't diminish your accomplishments. Enjoy them and look forward to the next win. The same thing goes for those solemn moments in your life. Allow yourself to absorb what's happening around you. Give yourself a moment and then move on. Dismissing or avoiding these critical moments in life will rob you of the joy or lessons that come with them.

I learned this the hard way. Unfortunately, I let many great moments pass me by without celebrating them because I was too caught up in trying to keep moving forward. I recall getting angry after actually reaching a goal. Why was I angry? Because I wasn't further along. Doesn't that sound ridiculous? I'd actually achieved a great milestone, and instead of celebrating that win and recognizing how far I'd come, I was looking at how much farther I still had to go. Instead of being excited, I felt frustrated. My accountability partner helped me snap out of it and reminded me of how much progress I had made. Don't cheat yourself. Enjoy the journey and take it all in because every experience matters.

Get your rest. Pace yourself. I recall days where I worked so hard it became difficult to think productively. My mind seemed foggy and my creativity waned. Despite running on empty, I continued pushing myself. I recall one particular time when I'd written several pages of a scene in one of my books. The writing was lackluster, flat, and didn't get to the point. I didn't want to read it so I knew readers wouldn't want to either. I ended up having to delete all that I'd written. I finally stopped pushing myself and rested. Once I was refreshed, my sense of creativity returned. Lack of rest will not only stunt your creativity, it will render you unproductive and make you unhealthy. What good is it to live your Dream Journey if you're too sick to enjoy it? Incorporate rest, wellness, and restoration into your work schedule.

Build yourself a library of great business books. Some of my favorites include, *The Go Giver,* by Bob Burg and John David Man, *Good to Great* by Jim Collins, the book *Instinct, Destiny* and *Soar* by Bishop T.D. Jakes, *The Hollywood Commandments* by Devon Franklin, *The Empress Has No Clothes* by Joyce Roche, *The Four Spiritual Laws of Prosperity* by Edwene Gaines, and *The Law of Success* by Napoleon Hill. Again, never stop learning.

Find your tribe. Spend time around the right people. Establish relationships with like-minded individuals. You should be able to share insights to help each other and support one another. Find people who are further along than you are and let their journey teach and inspire you.

Develop boundaries. When you do what you love, it's easy to blow past boundaries—especially in a work-from-home environment. Your work life can and will easily blend into other areas of your life. Work life balance is an oxymoron. It is a never-ending tug of war. Some days you will work more and others you should get a bit more rest. Find ways to transition from work to home life that gives your mind a few moments to settle down. Schedule down time if you need it and make sure you stick to it. If you're running your business from home, work with your family to create mental and physical boundaries that they respect to give you the space you need to work effectively.

Now, go make it happen and then get up every day, do what you love, and get paid for it. Most of all, enjoy the journey!

ACKNOWLEDGMENTS

As always, I must first give honor to God, my Lord and Savior Jesus Christ who is the head of my life. Thank you for this journey and the new chapters.

I must always thank my hubby, Les Flagler, and children, Les, Milan and Laila for being a constant inspiration and for always having my back. To my rocks, my siblings who keep me grounded, Cora, Valorie, Patricia, Eileen, and Rodney. Also my cousins who have been the forces behind me, Rebecca and Sharon, as well as a host of nieces and nephews. My family is the absolute best, and they are the reason I thrive and strive. They have always encouraged the dreamer in me.

A special thanks goes to the original Passionistas, the women who generously gave their time to discuss and explore some of the principles we talked about in this book. Thanks so very much to Darlene A. Anderson, Abiola Abrams, Dr. Michele C. Reed, Lutishia Lovely, Stacey Ciceron, Leslie Ware, Kellie Carpenter White, Karen Farnum-Williams, Wilma Holmes Tootle, Tricia Messeroux, Angelique Perrin, and Nyakio Grieco.

To all the dreamers out there, I can't wait to cross your path and see how you're soaring. Let's stay connected. Please join my email list by visiting my website at ReneeDanielFlagler.com and meet me on social media on Facebook, Instagram, Twitter, and LinkedIn.

ABOUT THE AUTHOR

Renee Daniel Flagler is an award-winning writer and business leader, a coach and speaker who is passionate about encouraging individuals and youth to pursue their passion and purpose. She is an advocate for empowering youth in the United States and abroad. She is also the Executive Director of Girls Inc. of Long Island whose mission is to inspire all girls to be strong, smart, and bold.

www.ingramcontent.com/pod-product-compliance
Lightning Source LLC
Chambersburg PA
CBHW051838040426
42447CB00006B/591